Leaving DarkLand *is a contribution towards realism in a day* Christian leaders are deceiving people with false expectations for the Christian experience. But it is also a message of hope for all of us who have experienced the failures and tragedies of life and get crushed by them. It is a biblical antidote for the gloom and doubt which Satan brings even upon the true children of God. I do not know of a book which has given such a comprehensive catalogue of the various negative emotions of true believers, how they affect God's people and how they can be managed. And it comes from a man who has walked a special road of grief and sadness. This book is more than just an abstract treatise for me for it was my responsibility and privilege to try to comfort Ed and his friends as I conducted the funeral of the precious little child which lay in state before us. A more poignant and yet important opportunity i have never experienced. For that shattered life of the friend who listened I sought, as best as I could, to bring comfort from Heb. 12:28 which speaks of a "Kingdom which cannot be shaken." It is my hope and prayer that **Leaving DarkLand** will help the suffering, afflicted people of God who live in the modern world to press on in serving the Lord, with the dynamic message of this book before them.

—**Dr. John F Thornbury**
Author and Retired Pastor

'Our theology must eventually become our biography. You will never know how strong the foundation of your faith is until walk through this DarkLand.' These sage-like words by my friend, Ed Wallen, describes a pilgrimage through the pain and grief precipitated by the loss of a loved one. In Ed's case, his beloved daughter was taken from this life way too early. Throughout the years since her death, Ed Wallen has been on a journey through the DarkLand of suffering and sorrow. As a fellow struggler in the grief process and as an author of a well-written book, Ed can be your human guide through the DarkLand of grief. This is not an easy road to travel but with the grace of God as your sustenance and with people of faith, like Ed Wallen, you will discover there is light at end of the DarkLand.

—**Dr. Rick Lance**
Executive Director of the Alabama Baptist State Board of Missions

Leaving DarkLand *is a deeply spiritual resource for the person facing difficulty of any nature and is a good reference for a pastor who may be preaching on the problem of pain, evil, and suffering. Ed Wallen masterfully addresses the subject. He introduces it with the most painful day of his life and draws upon his personal experience as well as decades of Bible study and pastoral ministry. It is biblically and theologically sound. The book was used by the Holy Spirit to encourage me. It is full of poems, hymn texts, and statements of saints of old. I thoroughly recommend this book. Reading it is good preparation for difficulties to come and encouragement and instruction for persons in difficulty.*

—**Dr. Hugh Richardson**
Director of Missions of the Shelby Baptist Association
of Alabama Baptist

'The gift nobody wants.' In a time when a proper theology of suffering, pain, and adversity is lacking, ***Leaving DarkLand*** *provides a much needed corrective to the popular false teaching on the subject. Contrary to the belief that God does not desire His children to suffer, Wallen first biblically, then practically and experientially shows the truth that God both ordains and uses suffering, pain, and adversity for the believer's good and for His own glory. If you are a pastor who at times struggles in counseling those who are experiencing suffering, pain, and adversity (and who doesn't!), along with the physical, mental and emotional states that often accompany (despair, discouragement, depression, fear, grief, anger) then you will profit greatly from this book. After all, pain is 'the gift nobody wants.'*

—**Pastor Todd Wilson**
Grace Covenant Baptist Church,
Vestavia Hills, Alabama

# Leaving DarkLand

How God's Instruction Manual Gives Effective
Prescriptions for Life's Most Difficult Problems

Ed Wallen

Foreword by Dr. Timothy George

Solid Ground Christian Books
PO Box 660132
Vestavia Hills AL 35266
205-443-0311
mike.sgcb@gmail.com
www.solid-ground-books.com

LEAVING DARKLAND

How God's Instruction Manual Gives Effective Prescriptions for Life's Most Difficult Problems

Ed Wallen

First edition January 2016

ISBN: 978-159925-356-5 (paperback)
ISBN: 978-159925-357-2 (hardcover)

© Copyright 2016 held by Ed Wallen. All rights reserved.

Cover design by Borgo Publishing in Tuscaloosa, Alabama. Contact them at borgogirl@bellsouth.net

Contents

Foreword .... *vii*
Preface .... *ix*

Introduction 1
Chapter 1: The Gift Nobody Wants 6
Chapter 2: Suffering 22
Chapter 3: Answers Attitudes and Actions 44
Chapter 4: Stress 62
Chapter 5: Failure 80
Chapter 6: Discouragement 94
Chapter 7: Portraits of Discouragement 113
Chapter 8: Depression 132
Chapter 9: Impatience 154
Chapter 10: Recognition 164
Chapter 11: Persecution 177
Chapter 12: Fear 192
Chapter 13: Death 202
Chapter 14: Grief 215
Chapter 15: Anger 230
Chapter 16: The King Says Come 244

This book is dedicated to
my wife **Tommie**, without whose
help this book would never be.
And, to our three grandchildren,
Noah, Macey, and Joseph

Foreword

Martin Luther once confessed: "I did not learn my theology all at once, but I had to search deeper for it, where my temptations [Anfechtungen] took me.... It is not understanding or reading or speculation that makes one a theologian. It is living, nay, rather dying and being damned that makes one a theologian." On another occasion, Luther summed up the Christian life in an even shorter statement: "Experientia facit theologum" (Experience makes a theologian).

Luther did not mean that personal experience was the basis or criterion for constructing or assessing theological statements. That view is at the root of modern subjectivism and theological liberalism. No, when a tree falls in the forest and crashes to the ground, it makes a sound whether there is anyone there to hear it or not. True theology is grounded on the objective truth of divine revelation in the Bible and in Jesus Christ. But when Luther says, "Experience makes a theologian," he is declaring that the truth revealed in the Spirit-inspired Scriptures must be personally appropriated, inwardly digested, and tested again and again on the anvil of daily life. "Thy words were found, and I did eat them," wrote the prophet Jeremiah (Jeremiah 15:16).

In 1986, Ed Wallen's beloved daughter, Susan, was killed in a tragic automobile accident. Two years later, in 1988, I moved to Birmingham, Alabama, to begin the work of Beeson Divinity School of Samford University. At that time, Ed was a pastor in the area, and we became good friends. Over the years, we have prayed together, travelled together, and ministered together. Ed's courage and spiritual integrity have shown through time and time again.

Ed's life was shattered by the death of his daughter and all that flowed from that event. In this book, he describes some of the pain he experienced. Sometimes "dark nights of the soul" can be devastating to one's faith and trust in God. Sometimes they can leave the sufferer seemingly forever suspended on the gallows of "Why?" and "Why me?" Ed certainly writes as one "acquainted with grief," the kind of grief from which we all want to hide our faces. But he also writes as one who lives by the promises of God. He writes as one who knows the truth of Psalm 139:11-12, which says, *"If I say, Surely the darkness shall cover me; even the night shall be light about me. Yea, the darkness hideth not from thee; but the night shineth as the day: the darkness and the light are both alike to thee"* (KJV). Christus Victor!

This is a book written "out of the depths" (Psalm 130:1). This is a great book because it is an honest book, one that deals with the deepest agonies of human life in the light of God's providential love and overcoming grace. And this is a work of genuine pastoral theology. No shepherd of God's flock should be without it. Tolle lege! "Take and read!"

—TIMOTHY GEORGE

Founding dean of Beeson Divinity School
of Samford University and general editor of
the Reformation Commentary on Scripture

Preface

Twas He who taught me thus to pray,
And He, I trust has answered prayer;
But it has been in such a way,
As almost drove me to despair! [1]

It was early in the morning on August 16, 1986, when I said good bye to my wife and eleven year old daughter Susan as they left our home in Alabama to visit grandparents in Kentucky before school began. Susan was our only living child; a son, Stephen, had died at birth. The day became dark and rainy as storms moved across the South. At 6:00 p.m. that evening my doorbell rang. I opened the door; a policeman was standing there. Life changed.

The life I had enjoyed and treasured cracked and shattered like a mirror in my mind as the policeman spoke of a car accident near Hazard, Kentucky; I should call the nearby hospital. The officer answered my questions with visible pain and difficulty; Susan didn't make it and my wife was critically injured.

Numbness. My own emotions flooded over me with the force of a black monstrous tsunami making thoughts difficult and fragmented. I crossed the street to the home of a pastor friend and asked him to make some phone calls for me. Friends met me at the church where I was pastor. More and more people began coming to the church, one of which was a physician. He contacted the hospital where my wife had been taken in Kentucky, and spoke directly with one of the doctors there. Because of her severe injuries, she would have to be air-lifted to a larger hospital in Lexington, Kentucky, which housed a trauma center.

The men of the church immediately made plans to drive me to Lexington. It was late at night when we began the long drive, arriving early the next morning. My wife was already undergoing surgery on her arms and legs. She was diagnosed with multiple injuries, including a severe concussion which resulted in brain damage. The doctors gave no assurance that she would live. The next day I traveled to Paintsville, Kentucky, where Susan had been taken. Sorrow beyond anything I could have imagined overwhelmed me as I held her for the last time.

I had to arrange for her funeral and burial back in Alabama. With the help of many caring, loving people, the arrangements were made. One service was held in Kentucky, where most of our relatives lived; then we took my Susan back to Alabama for a graveside service and burial. No more hugs and kisses, no more smiles and laughs, no more bedtime stories, no more new photos to put on my desk. I had heard "Daddy!" for the last time.

After Susan's burial, I spent days at the hospital in Kentucky until my wife could be transported back to Alabama. In the meantime, Bobby Allison (the race car driver) had called the church and offered to fly his plane up to Kentucky and bring her back to Alabama as soon as the doctors agreed to let her go. I'll never forget Bobby's kindness.

She remained hospitalized in Alabama for several weeks until finally released to go home. Her mental capacity had not recovered; in fact, it never did. She became extremely paranoid, accusative, hostile, etc., struggling with those problems for the remainder of her life.

I tell you all this to let you know that for all practical purposes I lost my entire family in that automobile accident. In the time it takes to turn a page, life as I knew it was in the past and gone. I had lost a little son twelve months earlier and now the rest of my family.

What I am writing is not theory but experience. I know what it is to suffer emotionally, to be discouraged, misunderstood, and to fight the tendency to become angry and bitter and depressed. But by *His* grace and mercy and strength I never lost faith in Christ my Lord, He never left my side, He never let go of my hand; I may have faltered, but He never did.

Yet I learned a lot about a place that everyone experiences in one fashion or another. Although, to some degree, living on this side of Heaven is living in a dark land, yet the path of life can take such severe and unexpected twists and turns that I must give it a unique name: DarkLand. It's a time in life where the clear light of our Great King may be obstructed or absent, the air can be thick and dismal, often confusing. Nevertheless, this DarkLand of aloneness is not outside of His domain and purpose. All is designed and allowed by Christ who knows exactly what is needful and when for each of His children. He walked through it Himself and has made for us a highway through its maze and wilderness.

I want to relate to you what God has to say in His Word to anyone who finds themselves in DarkLand—not a place of abandonment by God, but a place where the bright sunshine of joy has seemingly turned its face away. Although we all will walk in its shadows, DarkLand is not a place to camp and stay, but a place to learn and leave. There is only one source of real and lasting comfort: the King Himself, sovereign, loving, and compassionate; the Lord and Savior, Jesus Christ. In DarkLand He teaches us that all things serve Him. He has never disappointed me. William Cowper said it well when he wrote:

> That were a grief I could not bear,
> Didst thou not hear and answer prayer;
> But, a prayer-hearing, answering God
> Supports me under every load. [2]

---

1 John Newton, *Olney Hymnal*, Book III, #36
2 William Cowper, *Olney Hymnal*, Book III, #19

INTRODUCTION

> Heal us, Immanuel, here we are,
> Waiting to feel Thy touch;
> Deep-wounded souls to Thee repair,
> And, Saviour, we are such. [1]

C.S. Lewis wrote, "One road leads home and a thousand roads lead into the wilderness." [2] It seems that today as never before people are struggling with so many difficulties; to walk in the right path can be like climbing a rocky hill with biting wind in your face. Everywhere along this narrow path which God's people walk and do battle are countless side roads which promise an easier way through life. Although the path of life for the Christian is not easy, never turn aside. Turning away from God's will and God's road is always turning *to* something else which leads into the wilderness.

Difficult events and circumstances trigger stress, which can usher in discouragement and in many instances depression. Discouraged, disappointed, frustrated, financially burdened, depressed, "stressed out", angry, and uncertain about life now and the future describe the culture we live in. Tens of thousands of folks are frying their brains with all kinds of mind-altering drugs or numbing it with electronic games and gadgets, perhaps all done in the unrealized quest for peace of mind, escapism, or just to alleviate anxiety and fears. The drug industry is growing by leaps and bounds. Society in general is obsessed with the newest electronic gadgets; problems are not really being solved, just masked, peace seems elusive, and day to day living gets more complicated and fast-paced. A sad part of all this is that children are being swept up in it as well. Far too often kids are being medicated for doing what kids naturally do when they are undisciplined, or when they're just acting like children; more and more physicians and medical scientists are coming to the same conclusion.

At the same time, our society and even some who call themselves Christians scoff at the idea that the Bible has answers for these issues. The world tends to treat symptoms; God's Word through the Holy Spirit addresses and treats the root and cause of problems.

People who have lived for the past 50 years have seen an explosion of knowledge and technology; along with this massive explosion comes a mixture of emotions and reactions. Some want to believe that anything which makes life more comfortable and easy is a blessing. Thinking scripturally has become a foreign concept even in the church.

Media technology has transformed us into the most informed generation in the history of civilization. We can turn on our television at any time night or day and see what is going on in most every country in the world. We see starving, diseased, and poor people in what are called the third world countries. We see the dead where war is being waged. We hear the warnings of economic disaster in our own country. Rarely do we hear anything encouraging from the news media. Is it any wonder that people are living under stress and emotional pain and upheaval?

In the face of all this, have people come to believe that there are no real answers? In search of the way *out* of the dark, they turn *to* the dark. The pharmaceutical industry has been very successful in their pill pushing campaigns, even to the point of making us fearful of not taking a pill when we're healthy. In our society, most every difficulty is now labeled a disease, therefore "must" be treated with drugs. It's lamentable that many in the medical profession have bought into the pharmaceutical philosophy of a pill for every problem. But also, let me hasten to say that there is a minority, perhaps a small minority, of our population which *does* need treatment or some form of medication for the maladies discussed in this book.

The non-believer will find little comfort in this book. Although unbelievers can find some help in this book, *Leaving DarkLand* is written primarily for Christians who are struggling to know what God says about the problems they must contend with. God's Word has answers. *Leaving DarkLand* examines some difficult problems people face and points to the Bible, God's Word, for real help and healing. As we consider these life-wrenching subjects, understand that many are linked together—sometimes one fuels others. Where one problem is present, one or more of the other ills will most likely be close by ready to take on a "life of their own." Sparks from a fire can spread flames until an entire forest is ablaze.

Problems in life can be approached and dealt with in so many different ways, some good and some bad, some work and some don't. However, in this book I want to relate not only my own personal experiences but also those of others that I've counseled and spoken with over many years. Hurting people need real solutions, they need Light in the dark places of life, not man-made light but real Light from the Scriptures. The Lord is the Creator of man and He understands man better than anyone on this earth. His instruction manual, the Bible, gives us the effective prescriptions for life's most difficult problems. Prescriptions written by the Great Physician are exactly what I need and they will work for you as well. We must give ourselves over to Him completely and not quarrel with or spit out what He prescribes for us.

Some folks argue that relying on God's Word to guide us in everyday living and to solve problems is too simplistic. God's Word may be simply stated, but it is never simplistic. And faith in Him, though His gift to us, is made strong by its continual use. No Christian is made strong and mature by lifting "feathers."

> The life of faith seems so simple and easy in theory, that I can point it out to others in few words; but in practice it is difficult, and my advances are so slow,

> that I hardly dare say I get forward at all. It is a great thing indeed to have the spirit of a little child, so as to be habitually afraid of taking a single step without leading. [3]

As we go through these studies, remember, fellow Christian, that the Lord either allows or causes every event and circumstance that comes into your life; each one is an instrument to glorify God and mold you into the image of Christ. This is God's grand purpose and your ultimate destiny (Romans 8:28-29). Consequently, those events become *for you* a mirror in which to see yourself. You will either sit down in self-pity and bitterness in front of the mirror or the mirror will become a window through which you see the Providence of God, in love working all things for your good and His glory. As we take a look at the maladies and sorrows that you may experience in your life, let them become windows. The Word of God is powerful and He will guide you in wisdom, leading you out of the dark places of life. I want you to have full confidence in Christ the King and in the Scriptures. He provides the only effective armor suitable for the battlegrounds of DarkLand: wear it!

> O! I have seen the day, when with a single word,
> God helping me to say "My trust is in the Lord,"
> My soul has quelled a thousand foes,
> Fearless of all that could oppose.
>
> But unbelief, self-will,
> Self-righteousness and pride,
> How often do they steal
> My weapon from my side! [4]

Many ideas and concepts stated in this book are not completely original with me. I have read numerous sources on each of these subjects and have learned from great writers over the years. I have tried to cite these when I knew the exact source. Where I have failed to cite a source for an idea that I have written, I apologize. It certainly is not intentional. What I discuss in this book are things I have learned from personal experience, studying what others have written and shared, as well as the study of God's Word.

> What a poor, uncertain and dying world is this! What a wilderness in itself! Without the light of the Gospel and knowledge of Jesus—how dark, how desolate it is! It does not appear to us thus before we were saved—because we were then in a state of enchantment, the magical lantern blinding us with a splendid delusion!
>
> It is a great mercy to be undeceived in time; and though our mirthful dreams are at an end, and we awake to everything that is dismaying—yet we see a highway through the wilderness, and a powerful Guard, an infallible Guide at hand to conduct us through it! And we can discern, beyond the limits of the wilderness—a better land, where we shall be at rest and at home! [5]

---

1 William Cowper, *Olney Hymnal*, Book I, #14
2 C.S. Lewis, *The Pilgrim's Regress*, Book 8, p. 155
3 John Newton, *Cardiphonia*, Morgan and Scott LD, 1911, p. 195
4 William Cowper, *Olney Hymnal*, Book I, #17
5 John Newton, *The Works of John Newton, Volume 2*, Hamilton, Adams, and Co., 1820, reprinted by Banner of Truth Trust, 1988, pg. 229-230

1

THE GIFT NOBODY WANTS

You have tried us, O God;
You have refined us as silver is refined.
(Psalm 66:10)

God puts us in the fire of purification,
until His own image shines reflected in the gold! [1]

There's a Divine gift which everyone receives, but no one wants. It's a gift not sought, not requested, and rarely handled well. It is the gift of PAIN. While most do not desire it, pain is nevertheless a built-in safety feature of the body, similar to the lights on your automobile dash board which flash to alert that something is wrong or needs our attention. One of the great problems moms and doctors have is that a little baby cannot tell you where it hurts, but they know the baby is hurting because their safety valve activates: the baby cries. When you touch your finger to fire you immediately pull away because you feel pain. When you put your body in a twisted position, you feel pain. Pain is a messenger that tells you that something is wrong.

Suppose you could not feel pain. What would happen if you put your hand on a hot stove? Without pain, what would happen if you broke a leg or an arm? What if you could not feel the chest pains that signal a heart attack? Do you see how valuable the gift of physical pain is?

I once heard the story about a little girl in the state of Georgia who was afflicted with a very rare disease called "congenital insensitivity to pain with anhidrosis" (CIPA), a genetic disorder that renders her unable to feel pain. She must be watched constantly. Because she does not feel pain she doesn't know when she is injured; her food has to be tested to make sure that it's not hot enough to burn her mouth and or stomach. When she is at play, she has to be guarded to insure that she doesn't injure herself by breaking a leg or arm, etc. Unlike a little baby who cries when hurting, this little girl has no sensations of pain when injured. Her family lives in a state of constant fear and awareness of her inability to feel pain. If you were this little girl's family, what would you most likely be praying for? Would it not be that she could feel pain? Isn't it interesting that the very thing most people don't want and may be praying for its removal is one of the very things that is a life-saving gift from God: PAIN?

Leprosy *(Hansen's disease)* is a chronic infection caused by the bacterium Mycobacterium leprae. As you may know, this disease attacks the nervous system which often leads to the absence of pain in some parts of the body. Dr. Paul Brand was a world renowned expert on the disease of leprosy and was given a large grant to design an artificial pain system. He was looking for a way to help people who had lost the ability to feel pain, especially those suffering from leprosy.

In order to do this research Dr. Brand gathered a group of scientists: three professors of electronic engineering, one bioengineer, and several biochemists. After lengthy research, Dr. Brand, who was also a missionary, exclaimed: "Thank God for inventing pain! I don't think He could have done a better job. It's beautiful."

Dr. Brand's field of research was physical pain, but there are other kinds of pain: the pain of sorrow, grief, loneliness, fear, disappointment, depression, discouragement …the list is endless.

The society in which we live is a society in pain—high school students killing other students; at least one and one half million babies slaughtered each year by abortion (in the US alone); and thousands of suicides each year. We are a hurting society, in pain, physically, emotionally, mentally, and spiritually. That pain is telling us that something is amiss. Something is wrong. Something is not right. But instead of dealing with the cause, people think they ought to deaden the pain. Most people think they should never have pain. So what do they do? Drown the pain with alcohol. Deaden it with drugs. Pushing it to the corners of life and burying it by filling every minute with pleasures, sports, and entertainment.

Life in this world is full of pain because of the sinfulness of man. How we react and handle that pain is what determines how we get along in life. I am speaking to Christians. Christ is the only foundation capable of supporting you in times of ease and in times of pain; all imposters will crumble.

Christ is the starting place when faced with life's pain; seek Him first. We must trust in our sovereign King who either causes or allows pain in order to accomplish His purpose in us; that purpose is to make us like Himself (Romans 8:29). We must make our way through the painful experiences of life trusting fully in Him. We cannot always change our situation, but we can control the way we respond. Your circumstances may not be by choice, but your response is.

Our theology must eventually become our biography. You will never know how strong the foundation of your faith is until you walk through this DarkLand. There the distractions and glitter of the world are lost in the shadows and the superficial structures above the foundation may fall. I am saying this because when God puts His child in the fire, most of the things thought to be important and essential are burned up. Pain can either destroy you or build you up in your faith. It can make you better or bitter depending on the foundation of your faith and your response to that pain. Pain in whatever form it may come to you (physical, emotional, or spiritual) will either rule you or become your servant. Pain or circumstance does not form our character, but reveals true character. When the sun is shining brightly, it is easy to walk about without much effort and with a smile. But when the Lord allows us to step into a place in life where there is no light except Him, we find out a lot about our weaknesses, and a lot about His strength and grace.

We must learn how to cling, trust, and find joy in the midst of it all. Joy is a bit different than happiness. "Happiness" comes from the same root word as does "happenings." Happiness is actually based on happenings. You are happy when you get a new dress or your favorite team wins or you pay off your home or car, etc. Certainly there is nothing wrong with being happy as long as we understand that circumstances in life will not always produce happiness and even then it will be temporary. As circumstances change and shift, so follows "happiness."

Joy defies circumstances, and is the companion of peace. One can be at peace and have joy even in severe pain and void of happiness. Joy comes from the Lord. To know Him in His glory as our Lord and Savior and King brings a joy that no circumstance can diminish. Happiness is more of a feeling, but joy is rooted in attitude, knowing and resting in our posture, position, and place in Christ. Joy is that deep settled confidence that our sovereign Lord is in absolute control of every area of life. Joy is not dependent on circumstances; it is a choice. It's true, as some have said, "Pain is inevitable, but misery is optional." You cannot avoid pain, but you can avoid joy. You choose your attitude in any given circumstance.

Joy is free but not cheap. Happiness can be temporarily bought; joy comes free, yet has a high price tag. It comes with total commitment to Christ: *faith, faithfulness*, and *obedience*. You can be sure that our loving Lord will never lead one of his children to a place where His grace will not be provided. His grace is always sufficient.

Joy has more to do with who we are than what we have. Joy has more to do with health of attitude than health of body. Joy has to do with sacrifice vs. selfishness.

The apostle Paul often admonished believers to rejoice. Instructing the church at Philippi to be joyful even though there were problems, Paul wrote:

> *Rejoice in the Lord always; again I will say, rejoice! Let your gentle spirit be known to all men. The Lord is near. Be anxious for nothing, but in everything by prayer and supplication with thanksgiving let your requests be made known to God. And the peace of God, which surpasses all comprehension, will guard your hearts and your minds in Christ Jesus.* (Philippians 4:4-7)

Rejoice in the Lord
Notice carefully the source or place of rejoicing: "in the Lord." If you can't find something to rejoice in when you look to the Savior, you're a miserable, spiritually blind person. On the other hand, when your delight is in the Lord, His love, His grace, His mercy, His redemption, His promises, His presence, His power, His protection, and the prospects of His coming again, you have true Joy.

The joy that comes from blessings in Christ defies any difficult or painful circumstance in even the darkest of times. Paul said we are to rejoice "ALWAYS." And just in case you missed it the first time, he wrote: *"Again, I say rejoice."*

Excruciating pain may be accompanied by edifying joy. A suffering believer may see the Savior's face and smile. For the past several years I've traveled to Ukraine to minister to the Christians there and teach their pastors. One of our interpreter's mother is a brittle diabetic and in her early sixties. Already completely gray, her face is creased with wrinkles from a life of difficulty, her eyesight long gone, a leg amputated at the hip, and completely bed-ridden for over twelve years. However, each year we visit with her, she always blesses us with praising of her Lord, quoting precious scriptures and rejoicing in the Lord she loves. She demonstrates the attitude we should have when circumstances tempt us to mistrust, complain, and turn inward.

> Sooner or later, affliction and sorrow come to every Christian. We ought, therefore, to have true views about pain, about the divine reasons for sending it, and about the mission on which it comes. We ought to know, also, how to endure suffering so as to get from it the blessing, which its hot hand brings to us. [2]

The Reaction
There is an age old question: why do people suffer? There are only three reasons people suffer. Some suffering is because of our disobedience to the will of God. Some pain is for the glory of God, to expose Satan's big lie, which is that we obey God to gain His favor and therefore escape suffering. Some suffer as preparation for some special ministry.

Regardless of the reason or circumstances, you are to be gracious, patient, moderate, sweetly reasonable, courteous, and gentle. These are the opposite of being haughty, bitter, rebellious, and self-willed. Paul said, *"Let your gentle spirit be known to all men, the Lord is near"* (Philippians 4:5). What an encouragement. The Lord is present; if He is present, we can turn our thoughts toward Him in any situation and the light from His presence will cut through darkness and transform our thinking.

The presence of the Lord is of great comfort to anyone who is suffering pain, whether physical, mental, or emotional. Listen to this encouraging passage:

> *Though the fig tree should not blossom*
> *And there be no fruit on the vines,*
> *Though the yield of the olive should fall*
> *And the fields produce no food,*
> *Though the flock should be cut off from the fold*
> *And there be no cattle in the stalls,*
> *Yet I will exult in the Lord,*
> *I will rejoice in the God of my salvation.*
> *The Lord God is my strength,*
> *and He has made my feet like hinds' feet,*
> *And makes me walk on my high places.*
> (Habakkuk 3:17-19)

Warren Wiersbe has put this passage into contemporary terms as follows:

> Though the stock market crashes
> And there is no money in the bank;
> Though the supply of fuel dwindles
> And the machinery of society grinds to a halt;
> Though our ecological blunders ruin the crops
> And there are barren shelves in the markets;
> Yet I will rejoice in the Lord
> I will be joyful in God my Savior. [3]

That is what Paul is writing about when He admonishes us to rejoice always. If our delight is in the Lord, circumstances cannot rob us of that joy. So rejoice and react to adverse circumstances with an attitude of gratitude and kindness and trust.

> While they do not solve all the mystery of human suffering, the Scriptures show, at least, that suffering is no accident in God's world but is one of His messengers; and that it comes not as an enemy but as a friend on an errand of blessing. The design of God, in all the afflictions which He sends upon His people is to make them more holy, to advance their purification of character.
>
> It is very clearly taught in the Word of God, that suffering is necessary in preparing sinful souls in this world, for heavenly glory. "We must through much tribulation enter into the kingdom of God." There is no easy way to glory. There is so much evil in us, even after we are born again, that nothing less than the discipline of pain, can cleanse our nature. [4]

The Request
One characteristic of our society that stands out perhaps more than any other is that most people today worry about anything and everything. We live in a time of "what ifs." What if I had done this? If I had done that, would things be different, or better, or I would have prospered more?

People are worried about their health, death, the future, finances, the end times, and perhaps about the day they must stand before the Lord and give account for their life. However, Paul instructs the Christian to *"be anxious for nothing"* (Philippians 4:6). In other words, don't be worrying! After all, if the Lord is sovereign and we are His children, why should we be worrying over things that are in

His hands and purpose; besides, we can't change most of the things we worry about. God is sovereign over all things; *"For all things are Your servants"* (Psalm 119:91); and *"we know that God causes all things to work together for good to those who love God, to those who are called according to His purpose"* (Romans 8:28). Christians have been comforted by those words for over two thousand years; they are for you too.

Paul writes that we are to pray with specificity, mentioning by name what or who is on our heart and mind. Most prayers are too generic, covering a lot of things generally but nothing specifically. You have no doubt heard prayers like this: "Lord, bless all for whom it is our duty to pray." That sounds good, but it's certainly not specific, and probably ineffective. If there is someone you should be praying for, pray for them by name. Especially in your private prayer time be specific about what it is that you want the Lord to do for them.

> You are coming to a King,
> Large petitions with you bring.
> For His grace and power are such,
> You can never ask too much. [5]

The Apostle describes what our attitude should be when praying: *"but in everything, by prayer and supplication with thanksgiving let your requests be made known to God"* (Philippians 4:6). Whatever your request may be, it should be lifted to heaven by a heart of praise and thanksgiving. Praise and thanksgiving is that attitude we as Christians should have, even in pain and suffering. When we can thank the Lord for *everything,* we are acknowledging that He alone is God and Sovereign; we are bowing in confidence, with trust and reliance on His will. In so doing, we will be able to rejoice in the Lord regardless of the path that He allows, even through DarkLand.

Notice the reward Paul mentions in Philippians 4: *"And the peace of God, which surpasses all comprehension, will guard your hearts and your minds in Christ Jesus"* (v. 7). See how Paul puts all this together? In pain if we are rejoicing in the Lord, not worrying, but giving thanks for all things as we make our requests known to the Lord in prayer, then we will experience His peace which is beyond our ability to understand or produce. This joy and this peace cannot be taken from us, even though at times our heart may be filled with confusion.

Don't miss the remainder of the promise. Joy and Peace stand as sentinels to guard our hearts and minds. They guard against becoming bitter, difficult to get along with, cantankerous and rebellious. People who have these characteristics not only do not have joy, but they are unhappy, judgmental, haughty, critical, insecure, and likely to wound others. Paul says, *"Rejoice in the Lord"*; respond scripturally and, in faith, make your requests to the Lord with a thankful heart. He always fulfills His word, always!

> Tribulation is God's threshing, not to harm us or to destroy us but to separate what is heavenly and spiritual in us from what is earthly and fleshly. Nothing less than blows of pain will do this. Evil clings strongly, even to the godly. The golden wheat of godliness is so wrapped up in the chaff of the flesh that only the heavy flail of suffering can produce the separation. Godly character can never be attained, but through suffering. Holiness cannot be reached, without cost. Those who would gain the lofty heights must climb the cold, rough steeps which lead to them. [6]

The story of Joseph in Genesis gives us a scriptural portrait of a right response to adverse circumstances which cause us to suffer pain. He was the second-youngest of twelve brothers. Because of their father's evident favoritism to Joseph, his brothers became very jealous. One day they seized the opportunity to rid themselves of him; throwing Joseph into a pit they left him there to die. But in God's providence a band of traveling merchants came by, and the brothers sold him to those merchants who, in turn, sold him into slavery in the land of Egypt.

He was a slave in a foreign country; he was unable to speak the language; he was alone. To make things worse his master's wife accused him of rape; he was thrown into the miseries of an Egyptian prison; again he was alone and suffering. What was Joseph's attitude? We know that answer from the words that he spoke to his brothers many years later: *"As for you, you meant evil against me, but God meant it for good"* (Genesis 50:20). He knew all his pain and suffering was in God's purpose for he further said that it was *"to preserve many people alive."*

Joseph suffered; Joseph trusted God; the wheels of Providence moved at God's command, working all things out according to His good pleasure and His eternal purpose. That kind of mind-set lets the light shine brightly through the thick dark clouds of suffering and pain.

I once read a story of two seriously ill men who were placed in the same hospital room. The room was very small allowing only space for each man to hang a few clothes. There was only one window in the room. Their illnesses required that they remain quiet and inactive. They were not to listen to the radio, read a book or the paper, and certainly not watch television. They were together in this room isolated from the noisy activities of the other areas of the hospital. They enjoyed the quiet and spent most of their time talking about common things in their lives. They reminisced about growing up, families, work, vacations, and plans for the future.

The man next to the window was allowed to sit up for one hour twice each day, once in the morning and once in the afternoon. The other man had to lie flat most of the time. When the man next to the window was sitting up each day, he described what he saw outside. The other man could see in his mind all that was described to him: a beautiful park with a lake, children playing and throwing bread into the water to feed the ducks swimming in the lake. Other children were sailing their model sailboats along the edge of the lake. He could see the young couples walking hand in hand along the lake and through the trees. The grass was a deep green forming a background for the beautiful flowers which grew throughout the park. The old folks were seated on benches enjoying the children playing around them and feeding the pigeons. The man who was lying flat on his back began to look forward to the descriptions of the beautiful scenery outside the window by the other man's bed.

Then one day when the man was describing a parade, the other man began to think: Why should the man next to the window have this great privilege of seeing those beautiful sights? Why shouldn't I have the same privilege? The more he thought about it the more he wanted to move next to that window. After a few weeks he became bitter, reasoning that *he* should be beside the window. Becoming obsessed about the window he lay awake nights thinking about it. As his anger and bitterness grew, so also his illness worsened. The doctors expected that he should be getting better, but bitterness had stunted his recovery and the doctors were puzzled.

Then it happened. One night as he was lying awake staring at the ceiling, the man in the bed next to the window began to cough and struggle for breath. His lungs were congested with fluid and he gasped for breath and groped desperately for the button to call the nurses. But the other man watched and listened in silence.

The coughs became weaker and weaker. The struggle to breathe became fainter and fainter until there was silence from the man next to the window. He was dead, but the man next to him continued to stare at the ceiling.

The next morning the nurse came in and found the man dead. His lifeless body was quietly removed from the bed beside the window.

After a few days, the man in the room asked to be moved to the bed next to the window. His request was honored—they moved him and made him comfortable in his new bed next to the window. As soon as everyone was out of the room, in pain and discomfort, he raised himself up, propping on one elbow, and looked out the window anticipating the scene the other man had described so often; to his surprise all he saw was a BRICK WALL.

When it seems that you are facing a brick wall of circumstances, do you rejoice in the Lord and thank Him for all his blessings, or do you become bitter and resentful? One of these men had the right attitude—not complaining but rather seeking to encourage his fellow roommate. The other man became so bitter and self-focused that he let his friend die.

The man next to the window could find joy in the most difficult of circumstances; the other man may have died looking for circumstances which he thought would make him happy.

Let us be very careful that we do not fall into the error of complaining about something that is a gift of grace from our Lord. We should not spend our time examining the package the gift comes in, but the blessings it contains. The package may be anything that causes us pain or suffering, but the blessings inside may be many. Listen carefully to what an old faithful preacher and writer wrote about the sufferings in the lives of God's people. He mentions many of the blessings found inside the package of pain and suffering.

> "Be of good cheer: **it is I**; be not afraid." (Mark 6:50) Listen, then, to the voice of Jesus in the storm. **It is I** who raised the tempest in your soul, and will control it. **It is I** who sent your affliction, and will be with you in it. **It is I** who kindled the furnace, and will watch the flames, and bring you through it. **It is I** who formed your burden, who carved your cross, and who will strengthen you to bear it. **It is I** who mixed your cup of grief, and will enable you to drink it with meek submission to your Father's will. **It is I** who took from you worldly substance, who bereft you of your child, of the wife of your bosom, of the husband of your youth, and will be infinitely better to you than husband, wife, or child. **It is I** who have done it ALL.
>
> I make the clouds my chariot, and clothe myself with the tempest as with a garment. The night hour is my time of coming, and the dark, surging waves are the pavement upon which I walk. Take courage! **It is I.** Don't be afraid. **It is I**—your Friend, your Brother, your Savior! I am causing all the circumstances of your life to work together for your good. **It is I** who permitted the enemy to assail you, the slander to blast you, the unkindness to wound you, the need to press you! Your affliction did not spring out of the ground, but came down from above—a heaven sent blessing disguised as an angel of light clad in a robe of ebony.
>
> I have sent all in love! This sickness is not unto death, but for the glory of God. This bereavement shall not

always bow you to the earth, nor drape in changeless gloom your life. **It is I** who ordered, arranged, and controlled it all! In every stormy wind, in every darksome night, in every lonesome hour, in every rising fear, the voice of Jesus shall be heard, saying, "Be of good cheer: **it is I**; be not afraid." [7]

The Apostle Paul's view of pain and suffering is crucial in our life: *"I consider that the sufferings of this present time are not worthy to be compared with the glory that is to be revealed to us"* (Romans 8:18). Trying to weigh present suffering with future glory in heaven is useless. Our suffering in this life is temporal but the glory we will experience there is eternal. All the pain we could possibly endure on this earth cannot be compared to heaven. In reality the sufferings of this life prepare us for the glory in the next. As long as we are looking to Him who is all glorious, our light afflictions here are manageable.

Be very careful that you do not find yourself complaining about something God has given for your good and His glory. Our Father loves us just as we are, but he loves us too much to leave us as we are. So He often uses pain to mold us into the image of His Son.

But not all afflictions make people better. They do not always produce endurance. Chastening does not always yield the peaceable fruit of righteousness. We all have seen people suffering who became only more impatient, irritable, ill-tempered, and selfish as they suffered. Many a life in the furnace of affliction loses all the beauty it ever had. It is not by any means universally true that we are made more holy and Christ-like, by pain.

> Afflictions must be received as God's messengers. They often come in very somber garb, and it is only

when we receive them in faith, that they disclose to us their merciful aspect and mission.

We should therefore receive afflictions reverently, as sent from God. We may be assured that there is always some blessing for us, in pain's hot hand. There is some golden fruit, wrapped up in the rough husk. God designs to burn off some sins from us, in every fire through which He calls us to pass. No one who murmurs under God's chastening hand is ever made better by it. [8]

The *Olney Hymnal*, often cited, was published in 1779 and contained hymns written by John Newton and William Cowper.

1   J.R. Miller, gracegems.org/miller
2   Ibid.
3   Warren Wiersbe, *Looking Up When Life Gets You Down*, Baker Books, 2012, p. 34
4   J.R. Miller, gracegems.org/miller
5   John Newton, *Olney Hymnal*, Book I, #31
6   J.R. Miller, gracegems.org/miller
7   Octavius Winslow (1808-1878), gracegems.org/3/it_is_i.htm
8   J.R. Miller, gracegems.org/miller

2

SUFFERING

> Come to me O blessed trial, I need you.
> For you always draw me to the arms of the Savior. [1]

> There are no crown wearers in heaven
> that were not cross bearers on earth. [2]

Casualties of society are everywhere: the angry, the bitter, the depressed, the apathetic, the fearful, the guilt-ridden, and the lonely. No matter the description or the word used, they all spell SUFFERING.

If you were to take a tour back through the archives of the history of man, you would find the landscape cluttered with the skeletons of those who were broken by pain and suffering. Because of the fall of man into sin, there is no escape; *suffering is universal.* This is one truth and reality of life we must come to grips with if we expect to live a life, even as Christians, that is not shattered by afflictions. "Evangelical Christianity lacks a well-thought-out, Bible based, clearly articulated theology of suffering. If we had such a philosophy and acted on it, that would please God greatly and would be much to our spiritual and emotional benefit." [3]

We live in a sinful, spoiled and corrupted world; suffering goes with the system. Everyone may not have the same experiences, but everyone knows that *affliction* is a mighty huntsman with many different kinds of arrows: *disease, despair, depression, dis-*

couragement, rejection, failure, fear, loss, persecution, and a host of other sorrows. The book of Job teaches us well on the subject of affliction: *"man is born for trouble... Man, who is born of woman, is short-lived and full of turmoil"* (Job 5:7, 14:1). None escape the arrows sent or allowed by the Divine hand; for the Christian, each one is tipped with mercy and grace in the Savior's *purpose* and *providence*. Christians experience the sting of persecution because of their relationship to Christ; many suffer mightily because of their stand for Truth. Listen to what Peter wrote:

> *Beloved, do not be surprised at the fiery ordeal among you, which comes upon you for your testing, as though some strange thing were happening to you; but to the degree that you share the suffering of Christ, keep on rejoicing, so that also at the revelation of His glory you may rejoice with exultation. If you are reviled for the name of Christ, you are blessed, because the Spirit of glory and of God rests on you. Make sure that none of you suffers as a murderer, or thief, or evildoer, or a troublesome meddler; but if anyone suffers as a Christian, he is not to be ashamed, but is to glorify God in this name.* (1 Peter 4:12-16)

What do you do when suffering comes calling at your door? How do you remain faithful and trusting when everything seems dark and hopeless? Where do you turn and what do you do when you are made to feel weak, weary, wasted, and worthless? These are legitimate questions and we all must face them because we all will be visited by sorrow and suffering in some form. There are many paths to DarkLand, but the path of suffering is known by everyone. It can lead to the heart of DarkLand where the soul may wrestle with faith and sense no awareness of its great Friend's presence. Let us be cautious and pray for wisdom; in such a place as that, only God the Holy Spirit and His Word can light our way and take us out. We are helpless to generate light, not even a tiny spark.

I fear that we too often retreat to pious sounding phrases or clichés such as, "Keep your chin up, things have to get better." That sounds good, but it's not always true. Things often do get better, but many times they get worse. Another popular retreat is to quote part of Romans 8:28, *"We know that all things work together for good..."* (KJV). While this phrase certainly is true, it may not be very encouraging for someone in the midst of a severe crisis, suffering in soul, body and spirit, not seeing any light—only darkness.

Well, what do we do when Affliction calls on us? First, remove some myths from our thinking process.

Myths about Suffering and Affliction
Will you please go with me to the school of the Lord's Word and seek to understand *suffering* and *affliction* and observe it from God's point of view? It is on this very issue that skeptics and mockers camp, "How can there be a God when there is so much pain, suffering, and injustice in the world?" He has given us answers if we will search them out. When we comprehend a subject we can deal with it more effectively. Let God Himself speak to our minds from Scripture regarding this subject. Clear away long held myths which so often keep people entangled and make escape difficult. Falsehoods lead to bondage; Truth leads to freedom.

Myth No. 1: *All suffering and affliction are punishment for some sin.* Because of this myth, too often the first response to Suffering is, "Why am I being punished?" Jesus' disciples were victims of this erroneous thinking. John 9:2-3 records that while traveling with Jesus, they encountered a man who had been blind from birth. The disciples posed this question to Jesus, *"Rabbi, who sinned, this man or his parents, that he would be born blind?"* The answer Jesus gave must have stunned the disciples as it does people today. *"It was neither that this man sinned, nor his parents; but it was so that the works of God might be displayed in him."* In other words, this man was born blind so that Jesus might be glorified in his healing; Jesus gave him sight (as written in John 9). Am I saying that some suffering is providentially brought upon us by the Lord to accomplish His purpose and get glory to Himself? YES! That is exactly what I am saying because that is exactly what the Lord said. We must understand that God did not create this world, place men in it, and then run off and leave the world and us to make it on our own. He governs every event in this world and every event in the lives of men, *especially* His children. He has an eternal purpose and He either causes or allows events in His universe to accomplish that purpose. All suffering and affliction are not punishment or correction.

Let me pause to clarify: while all Suffering is not for punishment or correction, there are times when it is. We should always ask ourselves, "Is there sin in my life which brought about this suffering?" Certainly disobedience or neglect of our bodies can bring a lot of misery and affliction. For example, if a person becomes addicted to alcohol and damages their liver, suffering is going to occur because of both disobedience and neglect of the body. If parents neglect the discipline of their children, you can be certain the consequences of that sin will be sorrow and pain for both parents and children.

It is true that God uses affliction as an instrument of discipline; it is also true that not all afflictions come as punishment or correction. The righteous are persecuted and suffer, so be careful and patient when assessing others in their afflictions. Sometimes we suffer for righteousness sake. Jesus said:

> *Blessed are those who have been persecuted for the sake of righteousness, for theirs is the kingdom of heaven. Blessed are you when people insult you and persecute you, and falsely say all kinds of evil against you because of Me. Rejoice and be glad, for your reward in heaven is great; for in the same way they persecuted the prophets who were before you.* (Matthew 5:10-12)

Myth No. 2: *Affliction is nonproductive.* We live in a society that is happiness driven and emotionally oriented: a world of pleasure seekers, pleasure collectors, and pleasure lovers. Pleasure is the objective of life and consequently all unpleasant experiences are deemed unproductive. This philosophy gives birth to the idea that God created us to always be happy and feel good; there should never be anything in our lives that would keep us from always being delighted and happy; consequently, "all pain is bad and therefore unproductive." The Bible clearly stands in opposition to such a philosophy.

> *And not only this, but we also exult in our tribulations, knowing that tribulation brings about perseverance; and perseverance, proven character; and proven character, hope; and hope does not disappoint, because the love of God has been poured out*

within our hearts through the Holy Spirit who was given to us. (Romans 5:3-5)

Consider it all joy, my brethren, when you encounter various trials, knowing that the testing of your faith produces endurance. And let endurance have its perfect result, so that you may be perfect and complete, lacking in nothing. (James 1:2-4)

Christ knows us so much better than we know ourselves. He loves us so much that whatever is needed for our good He does not withhold, even when that "good thing" needed comes in the form of suffering. Our Good Shepherd desires that His sheep stay close to Him; it's there they are most safe and aware of Him. He uses the rod to protect and to teach. Trials and afflictions are necessary so that "they should learn not only what *He* can do for them—but how little *they* can do without Him!"[4]

Myth No. 3: *Affliction and suffering are signs of spiritual failure.* The implication is that the absence of affliction is a sign of God's blessing and the presence of affliction is a sign of unfaithfulness. This is a popular belief in many modern day American pulpits. But, is this a Scriptural concept? If affliction and suffering are signs of spiritual failure and unfaithfulness, why did God's faithful servants suffer—Paul, Peter, James, John? A considerable list is presented in Hebrews chapter eleven of God's servants who endured tremendous hardships, agonies and even death. It would be foolish to argue that all these people were unfaithful and spiritual failures, when in fact they were spiritual heroes.

Myth No. 4: *Affliction and suffering are incompatible with a God who is good and loving and all powerful.* This myth reveals a total lack of knowledge about God, the Fall of Man and its ramifications, and Satan. Because of the Fall of Man, the entire world is under a curse which involves pain and suffering. The fabric of life in this world is laced with dark tapestries; for the beloved of Christ, those threads have reason and function, serving His purpose to bring to light and to reveal the golden pattern and final image. *"We know that God causes all things to work together for good to those who love God, to those who are called according to His purpose"* (Romans 8:28).

These myths must be removed from your thinking. God does not change; His Word does not change. The myths are fast growing vines that hinder and entangle as we seek the face of our great King and Friend while we struggle in the dark places in life. Only Truth, the Sword of the Spirit which is the Word of God, can cut through. John Newton wrote:

> "Lord, why is this!" I trembling cried,
> "Will You pursue Your worm to death?"
> "This is the way," the Lord replied,
> "I answer prayer for grace and faith."
> "These inward trials I employ,
> From self and pride to set you free;
> And break your schemes of earthly joy,
> That you may seek your all in Me!" [5]

The Source of Affliction and Suffering

In the beginning God's creation was an unspoiled environment of perfection; free of all affliction, pain, trouble and suffering. All of creation was a revelation and reflection of the Creator, from the heavens, (sun, moon, stars, etc.) to earth and every creature on the earth—especially man who was made in the very image of God the Creator. Both the Old and the New Testaments deliberately root themselves back into the early chapters of Genesis, insisting that they are a record of human events. [6]

It is in Genesis where we read the account of our own beginning: our origin is in Adam, created in the image of God. Man was magnificent, beautiful, and intrinsically brilliant.

It was into this pristine and wonderful environment—a creation that reflected the Glory of God Himself—that Adam was created and placed. He was given dominion over earthly habitations, the birds of the air, the fish of the sea, and all animals on earth. We know nothing of the grandeur and perfection recorded in Genesis chapters one and two; it was into that exquisite garden of splendor that Adam and Eve were placed. In this painless, trouble-free, beautiful home man was endowed with freedom to love and obey God unhindered by a sin nature. Such a true freedom man has never enjoyed since that day when sin and corruption infused both mankind and the universe. And, that joyous and perfect state will not be experienced completely again until the Lord and Creator returns and makes all things right. Further, the last will be better than the first.

In that element of freedom given to Adam and Eve lay the potential in man for rebellion, disobedience, and failure. Sadly, man exercised that potential and disobeyed His Creator, fell into sin, and became a failure. Was it God who failed? No! God is no more a failure than is a teacher who gives a test with a potential for failure by the students. When Adam chose to sin, he fell from his created state and transferred his loyalty from God to Satan who immediately established himself as the god of this world (see 2 Corinthians 4:4). The earth changed; the universe changed; man changed. Sin had entered with its perversions of good and degenerative sludge that flowed through all that God had pronounced "good." Satan gained this control by controlling man; the creation itself groans as a result (Romans 8:18-23).

Since that event in the Garden of Eden, both the human race and the creation have been plagued by affliction and suffering. Sin is the ultimate source of suffering and Satan was the original source of sin. As soon as sin hit the scene, just as God had warned, it brought spiritual death and all the miseries, troubles, blindness, and depravity associated with it. Note what happened to man when Adam fell.

> Man lost his relationship with his Creator
> Man's relationships became selfish
> Man lost self-esteem (Genesis 3:7)
> Man experienced shame and alienation (3:8)
> Man became full of fear (3:10)
> Man became dishonest (3:12)
> Woman suffered pain in childbearing (3:16)
> The earth was cursed (3:17)
> Man would have to toil in futility until he died (3:17-19)

Because of sin, by the time Genesis 4 is concluded, Adam and Eve had suffered terribly. Not only had they suffered the loss of fellowship with God and the paradise of the Garden, but now they experienced the trauma and consequences of jealousy between their sons: anger, murder, and the violent loss of a child. The first man and woman now lived in a godless society, the sad and heart-rending consequences of their sin.

The Bible consistently and persistently attributes the source of suffering to Satan and sin; however, only by God's approval can affliction come upon His redeemed people. Job's bitter miseries came from Satan by God's permission. Paul's thorn in the flesh came from Satan as an instrument of God (2 Corinthians 12:7). Make no mistake about it, Satan delights to inflict pain and misery on the people of God; it is one way he attempts to denigrate the glory of God, at least in the great Deceiver's own mind.

Satan is skillful and successful in his work of causing pain and suffering. When was the last time you heard Satan blamed for war, poverty, starvation, and crime? Who gets the blame for murder, rape, greed, troubles, afflictions, etc.? Most people say that the source of these things is genetics, society, or environment. Satan and sin never seem to get the blame. Certainly the Lord is not passive in these maladies since Satan can only do what the Lord allows as illustrated in the case of Job; from an earthly perspective the main cause of our troubles is Satan and our personal sin. Fallen man is the instrument Satan uses to bring havoc on God's creation.

We must be constantly aware that Satan and sin will stick their ugly heads up in the most unexpected circumstances. For example, Righteousness itself will bring affliction and suffering. Listen to what Jesus told his disciples: *"These things I have spoken to you, so that in Me you may have peace. In the world you have tribulation, but take courage; I have overcome the world"* (John 16:33). The apostle Paul wrote, *"Indeed, all who desire to live godly in Christ Jesus will be persecuted"* (2 Timothy 3:12).

And from what source does this persecution proceed?—a fallen world under the dominion of Satan and inhabited by sinful and depraved men. The Righteous will always suffer because of the world's natural aversion to Christ's righteousness which God's children reflect. We also suffer in this world because of our own sinfulness; Satan is the master of using our sinfulness to bring about pain and suffering. Charles Spurgeon wrote, "Even on the best roads—we falter! In the smoothest paths—we quickly stumble! A straw may trip us up—and a pebble can wound us!" [7] But take courage and stand firm in Christ, knowing that our Loving Lord causes all things, (affliction and suffering included) to work for our good and His glory. When the path is dark and sorrows engulf, remember that Salvation was purchased by *Christ's* pain and suffering, and His presence is promised to us in our suffering.

The Solution to Pain and Suffering
Are you thinking, "If God is so good, loving, and powerful, why doesn't He do something about our suffering?" The answer is, "He has and He does!" Read it again: *"In the world you have tribulation, but take courage; I have overcome the world"* (John 16:33). Christ has already overcome the world through His death and resurrection. Satan, sin, and death were defeated.

> *O death, where is your victory? O death, where is your sting? The sting of death is sin, and the power of sin is the law; but thanks be to God, who gives us the victory through our Lord Jesus Christ.*
> (1 Corinthians 15:55-57)

As a result of Christ overcoming the world in His death, burial, resurrection, and ascension, our future is guaranteed; we are *"...sealed in Him by the Holy Spirit of promise"* (Ephesians 1:13). Someday Satan and his entire host will be cast into the lake of fire; the old heaven and old earth will be replaced by a new heaven and a new earth free from sin, sorrow, pain, and suffering. Our Savior and King will take His redeemed Bride into an eternal bliss. (See Revelation 21:1-8.) No afflictions, no confusion, no suffering, no shadow lands, no DarkLand.

Suffering is temporary for the redeemed. We, like Paul, can say: *"For I consider that the sufferings of this present time are not worthy to be compared with the glory that is to be revealed to us"* (Romans 8:18). Christ has given us the solution. He has overcome the world by death and resurrection and guaranteed the future—a future of painless life for all those who trust Him.

With all this in mind, how do we deal with the present? Because of His triumphant work, Jesus provides three dynamics which equip us with the capability and the means to prevail over the problems of the present.

First, He gives us His enabling grace. In his struggling with the agony of a thorn in the flesh, Paul learned that God's grace was truly sufficient to sustain him in the midst of that affliction. He learned to rejoice in Christ's power, wisdom, and grace; he was provided for and God was glorified even through the suffering. The Lord did not do away with the "thorn" even though Paul prayed earnestly and persistently that it would be removed.

> *Because of the surpassing greatness of the revelations, for this reason, to keep me from exalting myself, there was given me a thorn in the flesh, a messenger of Satan to torment me—to keep me from exalting myself! Concerning this I implored the Lord three times that it might leave me. And He has said to me, "My grace is sufficient for you, for*

> *power is perfected in weakness." Most gladly, therefore, I will rather boast about my weakness, so that the power of Christ may dwell in me. Therefore I am well content with weakness, with insults, with distresses, with persecutions, with difficulties, for Christ's sake; for when I am weak, then I am strong.* (2 Corinthians 12:7-10)

In this life, hurts and sorrows may not always be removed. But we are His and He never forgets His children, nor neglects His business.

> He often takes a course for accomplishing His purposes, directly contrary to what our narrow views would prescribe. He wounds in order to heal, kills that He may make alive, casts down when He designs to raise, brings a death upon our feelings, wishes, and prospects, when He is about to give us the desire of our hearts. These things He does to prove us; but He Himself knows, and has determined beforehand what He will do...He is still working wonderfully for us, causing light to shine out of darkness, and doing us good in defiance of ourselves. [8]

The grace and Word of God mark the way we must walk in the light and in the dark. Trust in the truth of His word brings strength in weakness and glory to His Name.

> *When you pass through the waters, I will be with you; And through the rivers, they will not overflow you. When you walk through the fire, you will not be scorched, nor will the flame burn you.* (Isaiah 43:2)

> Through many dangers toils and snares
> I have already come.
> Tis grace has brought me safe thus far,
> And grace will lead me home. [9]

A second dynamic is the glory of God. His glory often comes shining in at the darkest hours of our lives to lift us up and support us. Hymn writer Fanny Crosby was blinded by a careless physician when she was a small child, but she wrote over 10,000 hymns. In her blindness the glory of God shined into her soul and is reflected in her words.

Another case in point is that of William Cowper, a man plagued with depression and deep despair throughout his entire life. He attempted suicide on multiple occasions. At one point Cowper was put into an asylum for the insane, but in God's providence, the man in charge of the institution was a Christian and became instrumental in William Cowper's salvation. God also provided His troubled servant with a great pastor, mentor, and friend, John Newton. Newton was known for his loving pastoral abilities and was the author of the beloved hymn *Amazing Grace* and hundreds of others. The two friends, Newton and Cowper, worked together for years writing hymns which were published as the *Olney Hymnal*. These two men are each shining proofs of God's providential work resulting in the glory of God. Christ delights in turning the tables on Satan who seeks to defame the name of Christ by attacking His people.

There is yet a third dynamic of encouragement: the body of Christ, the Church. Through His people, the Lord puts His arms around us to comfort us in our suffering.

> *Blessed be the God and Father of our Lord Jesus Christ, the Father of mercies and God of all comfort, who comforts us in all our affliction so that we will be able to comfort those who are in any affliction with the comfort with which we ourselves are comforted by God.* (2 Corinthians 1:3-4)

Through His Church, His redeemed people, Christ has provided an agent of comfort for those who are suffering. I remember well the cards, letters, phone calls, and visits that I received after my daughter's death. All were very comforting, knowing that people in numerous churches and in many states cared enough to express their sorrow and their promises to pray for me and my wife. My own church where I was pastor made every provision to comfort me physically, emotionally, and spiritually. Those days were extremely difficult, but God, by His grace through His church, provided that human comfort that was essential for me to make it through those days.

The grace, glory, and body of Christ do not always remove the troubles or the suffering we experience, but they always give strength and purpose for endurance and perseverance. In the present, we have His grace, His glory, and His Church to encourage, strengthen, and comfort us in our trials in this life. That is exactly what John Newton did for his friend William Cowper who, in an hour of distress, wrote:

> God moves in a mysterious way,
> His wonders to perform;
> He plants His footsteps in the sea
> And rides upon the storm.

> Deep in unfathomable mines
> Of never-failing skill,
> He treasures up His bright design,
> And works His sovereign will.
>
> Ye fearful saints, fresh courage take;
> The clouds you so much dread
> Are big with mercy, and shall break
> In blessings on your head.
>
> Judge not the Lord by feeble sense,
> But trust Him for His grace;
> Behind a frowning providence
> He hides a smiling face.
>
> His purposes will ripen fast,
> Unfolding every hour;
> The bud may have a bitter taste,
> But sweet will be the flower.
>
> Blind unbelief is sure to err,
> And scan His work in vain;
> God is His own interpreter,
> And He will make it plain. [10]

The Divine Person and Purpose in Suffering

There are two golden threads of truth entwined with suffering which make the difference between the world's children and Christ's Bride. Those Truths are: there is a divine Person associated with affliction and suffering; and that divine Person has a divine Purpose in all things. If, in the arena of affliction and agony, our minds can get a handle on these two truths, we will think rightly concerning pain and suffering. In Christ is all wisdom for right thinking and wise actions (see Colossians 2:3, Proverbs 1).

First, the Divine Person is, of course, Jehovah God: *omnipotent* (all powerful), *omniscient* (all knowing), and *omnipresent* (everywhere present). His attributes give solid ground for encouragements. The God of the Scripture is sovereign; He stands guard over the lives of His people. Every pain, every stumble is either by divine action or permission—nothing is accidental with the Lord. Christ the King stands like a sentinel at the gates of our existence and allows nothing to pass into our lives without His approval and for His Purpose. Satan had to obtain God's permission before he could touch Job or his family (see Job 1:6-12). The same was true with Peter: *"Simon, Simon, behold, Satan has demanded permission to sift you like wheat, but I have prayed for you, that your faith may not fail..."* (Luke 22:31-32). Remember this, whatever Christ prays for in His humanity, He will grant in His deity. His prayers for His people cannot go unanswered. In John 17, Christ prays that the Father will keep all those who had been given by the Father to Him, that they would be united, that they might have His joy fulfilled in themselves, that they be kept from the evil one, that they be sanctified in truth. All of His prayers will be answered, regardless of circumstances which God, in His divine Providence, allows or sends our way.

Even though all affliction and suffering comes by divine permission and even though all suffering has its ultimate source in the activities of Satan and sin, different doors of experience may be used for suffering's entrance into our lives. It may be caused directly by Satan, as with Job; some people suffer because of the disobedience or carelessness of others, as with Joseph; some suffer because of personal disobedience, as with Jonah. Sometimes misery and fear come because God creates the circumstance for the affliction, as with the stormy seas (see Mark 4:35-41). Perhaps a combination of all of these things brings "the Perfect Storm of Misery." Whatever the second cause is, God is still King over our affliction and suffering and is therefore the First Cause. As our Lord said, *"Are not two sparrows sold for a cent? And yet not one of them will fall to the ground apart from your Father. But the very hairs of your head are all numbered"* (Matthew 10:29-30).

Would it not be terribly frightening to think that God did not know of our afflictions and had no control over them? But He does know and He does control all the pain, miseries, and darkness that come into our lives; He also controls the things which we label as good. If anything comes from His hand to us, is it not for our good?

Christ the God Man is Sovereign and He changes not. His attributes do not vary or alter; He cannot violate His nature. The Lord cannot be unfaithful. He is Truth, therefore cannot lie (2 Samuel 7:28). He is eternal, therefore cannot die. He cannot deny Himself (2 Timothy 2:13). He does not choose to exist—HE IS. He does not choose to love, He is the God of love. He does not choose to be merciful—He is the God of mercy. He does not choose to be just—He is the God of Justice. All His attributes are intrinsic to His Being of Holiness and Glory, these are His Nature. His intrinsic nature guarantees that all the suffering that He allows into the lives of His people works for their good. He is never malicious or wrong in what He causes or permits. His goodness, power, justice, and holiness are gardens of refuge and comfort to His children when they suffer. The truths about the goodness and all other attributes of Christ are forever true and stand firm in every place—even in DarkLands.

Whatever may be the immediate causes of your troubles—they are all under the direction of a gracious hand—and each, in their place, cooperating to a gracious end. Your afflictions all come from God's heart, who loves you better than you love yourself! They are all tokens of His love and favor—and are necessary means of promoting your growth in faith and grace. [11]

> *The Lord is righteous in all His ways*
> *and kind in all His deeds.*
> (Psalm 145:17)

Second, the Divine Purpose. Purpose always alters our perspective, especially in times of affliction and hurt. When convinced that the gain will be worth the pain, we rest in Him and can react scripturally and have assurance in Him our Savior. We are convinced of this only when we recognize that God has a definite purpose in our life, in our nation, in our world, in history, in the universe and in all that is. Purpose always alters our perspective on suffering. Paul expressed this truth when he wrote:

> *Therefore we do not lose heart, but though our outer man is decaying, yet our inner man is being renewed day by day. For momentary, light affliction is producing for us an eternal weight of glory far beyond all comparison, while we look not at the things which are seen, but at the things which are not seen; for the things which are seen are temporal, but the things which are not seen are eternal.* (2 Corinthians 4:16-18)

Are you convinced that sorrows and sufferings have a divine purpose for you? If so, you will not rely on pagan axioms, like "Grin and bear it," or "Look for the silver lining," or "You have to pull yourself up by your own bootstraps!" and the most popular one, "Think positively!" Those little clichés may sound instructive, but not a one of them will help you endure real darkness and suffering because they have the wrong perspective. Thomas Watson, an old Puritan preacher and writer said it well when he wrote:

> God gives affliction to purge our corruption...God sanctifies all our afflictions. They shall not be destructive punishments, but medicines! They shall corrode and eat out the venom of sin! They shall polish and refine our grace! The more the diamond is cut—the more it sparkles. The more God afflicts us—the more our graces cast a sparkling luster! [12]

A few years ago when the University of Kentucky was playing for the NCAA championship in basketball, I came home just in time to see the final few minutes of the game on television. I sat there anxious and wrapped up in the game since I'm a Kentucky Wildcat fan. Sure enough Kentucky won the game. Later, on another channel, I watched the replay of the entire game. I sat back all relaxed. Why the difference? Knowledge! I knew the end result. And knowing that suffering as a Christian has a divine purpose certainly makes a difference in how we act in times of aching and hurting. As a child of God, we know the end results.

When Paul found out there was a purpose for his thorn in the flesh, he rejoiced in his infirmity (2 Corinthians 12:10). He understood that his suffering was for the glory of God.

The Christian lives on hope. I am not talking about some shallow and subjective form of wishful thinking which is far removed from reality. I fear that too many people have some sort of a Pollyanna view of life in general. The Hope I am writing about is not some pipe-dream which has no basis or true foundation. The hope the Christian lives by is based solidly on the promises of God contained in His word. We are looking forward to the fulfillment of those promises when our sufferings and strivings will cease; light will shine eternally and we will understand it all. *"And He will wipe away every tear from their eyes; and there will no longer be any death; there will no longer be any mourning, or crying, or pain; the first things have passed away"* (Revelation 21:4). I want to be numbered with that group of people, don't you?

> The path of affliction is sanctified by the promises of God, and by the consideration of our Lord Jesus, who walked in it Himself, that we might not think it too much to tread in His steps. Yes, it has been a beaten path in all ages; for the innumerable multitudes of the redeemed who are now before the eternal throne, have entered the kingdom by no other way. Let us not then be weary and faint—but cheerfully consent to be the followers of those who, through faith and patience, are now inheriting the promises! [13]

> *It is good for me that I was afflicted,*
> *that I may learn your statutes.*
> (Psalm 119:71)

God does not create in our heart any hopes which He does not fulfill, any longings which He does not satisfy, and any aspirations which He does not complete. Suffering always precedes glory. First comes the darkness of Good Friday, then the blazing light of Resurrection Sunday.

---

1 George Whitefield, gracegems.org/3/it_is_i.htm
2 Charles Spurgeon, www.spurgeongems.org
3 Alistair Begg, *Made For His Pleasure*, Moody Press, 1996, p. 107
4 John Newton, gracegems.org/newton/additional_letters_of_newton.htm, Letter #6
5 John Newton, *Olney Hymnal*, Book III, #36
6 Francis Schaeffer, *Genesis in Space and Time*, Vol. II, Book I, Crossway Books, 1985
7 Charles Spurgeon, Spurgeon Gems, Vol. 1, gracegems.org
8 John Newton, *Cardiphonia*, Morgan and Scott LD, 1911, p. 165
9 John Newton, *Olney Hymnal*, Book I, #41
10 William Cowper, *Olney Hymnal*, Book III, #15
11 John Newton, gracegems.org/09/08/afflictive.html
12 Thomas Watson, *Ten Commandments*, Banner of Truth Trust, 1959
13 John Newton, gracegems.org/09/08/afflictive.html

On Friday, January 1, 1773, an hour or two after hearing Newton preach at the morning service in church, Cowper was walking in the fields around Olney when he was struck by a terrible premonition that the curse of madness was about to fall on him again. Struggling to make a declaration of his faith in poetic form before his mind was enclosed in the darkness of depression, he struggled home, picked up his pen, and wrote a hymn that many regard as a literary and spiritual masterpiece.

> God moves in a mysterious way,
> His wonders to perform;
> He plants his footsteps in the sea,
> And rides upon the storm. (6 verses)

Soon after writing these memorable lines, the "dreaded clouds" arrived, and Cowper's mind plunged in an abyss of madness."

John Newton: From Disgrace to Amazing Grace, Jonathan Aitken; 2007, Crossway Books, pgs. 217-218

3

ANSWERS, ATTITUDES, AND ACTIONS

There are three things that make a man of God:
Supplication, Meditation, Tribulation. [1]

Those who dive in the sea of afflictions
bring up rare pearls. [2]

One of the great mysteries of human life is the mystery of pain, suffering and evil. Man is bewildered by the contemplation and experience of pain. "Why? Why has sorrow come to me? Why am I sick? Why are some handicapped? Why does death come to even the most innocent? Why disappointments; why shattered dreams; why failures?" There is pain in our bodies, pain in our minds, and pain in our hearts. Why must it be that way? "Why do the righteous suffer?" C.S. Lewis replies to that question: "Why not? They're the only ones who can handle it." [3] In times of sorrow and suffering, do we really have the right to ask the Lord, "Why is this happening to me?" *unless* we are willing to ask the same question in times of blessing and happiness.

Every possible blessing is also a possible source for pain. Love brings some of the greatest of joys into our life, yet also some of life's most aching and deepest sorrows. Love cost the Savior His life's blood, but His death is *our* greatest blessing. Pain is often the price paid for love. How many mothers have grieved many years over a wayward child? Why is she grieving? She grieves because of her love for that child.

Life's possibilities come in pairs: short and tall, strong and weak, hot and cold, black and white, pain and pleasure, good and evil. The existence of one carries with it the possibility of the other.

In times of affliction and darkness our thinking process is so often out of calibration like a telescope that is out of focus. God's thoughts are not our thoughts; there are many secret things which are not revealed to us. *"The secret things belong to the Lord our God, but the things that are revealed belong to us and to our children forever, that we may do all the words of this law"* (Deuteronomy 29:29). Too often Christians see life in individual segments only and assume that God ought to deal with us based on our own individual acts. Human beings often make judgments of what is good and what is bad based on our limited personal knowledge and assessments, thus thinking that God should punish or bless based on what one has personally done. If this was the basis on which God operated, we would all be in hell; we deserve nothing from the hand of God, except His justice. No one who suffers is innocent; no one is blessed solely on what they have or have not done. MERCY is *not getting* what we *do* deserve; GRACE *is getting* what we *do not* deserve. Both have been purchased through the blood of Christ, certainly not merited by anything found within the creature.

Previously we addressed *myths* associated with pain, the *source* of pain and suffering, the *solution* to pain and suffering, and the *divine Person and purpose* for pain and suffering. As a result of the above myths, there are three issues about which we must think correctly and scripturally: *answers, attitudes,* and *actions.* Affliction and suffering are always attended by these. They are never far away, but fakes and deceivers are never far away either. Let us scripturally examine these three reactions to affliction and suffering. It is crucial that our thinking be correct. Right answers, right attitudes, and right actions and results do not exist apart from the Bible and the God of the Bible.

Some Answers

Most all other questions about sorrow and suffering are contained in this one word question—WHY? Pain and suffering are universal and so is the heart cry to understand WHY. Having Biblical insights into WHY suffering exists will help us rightly deal with it in our own life.

Suffering: Temporal Judgment on Sin

When the Judge's gavel falls, time is up; the verdict is decided and the penalty is imposed. As unpleasant as it is to think about judgment, Christians must acknowledge that some suffering is directly related to sinful activities; some suffer because the gavel of Justice has hammered down and temporal judgment has been imposed. If we are living foolishly, if we are neglecting our bodies, if we are neglecting our minds, we are going to suffer consequences. If we abuse our bodies, the gavel will fall and suffering will come in one form or another. Likewise, when we neglect our spiritual responsibilities to the Word of God, we should not be astonished when that offense brings about an express passage to DarkLand.

When David sinned by an improper relationship with Bathsheba, and then had her husband Uriah killed by ordering him to the frontline of battle, David suffered tremendously. His infant son died. Turmoil came to live in David's household. His beloved son, Absalom, became his enemy. David suffered greatly. Psalm 51 expresses his heart cry in the loss of the joy of God's salvation (Psalm 51:12). The heavy cloud of judgment obscured the face of God. Salvation was not lost, but joy was hidden from David. His judgment was temporal not eternal. As the Puritan Thomas Watson says, "Affliction may be lasting, but it is not everlasting."

In the Old Testament scriptures, catastrophic events such as earthquakes and floods were acknowledged to be from God, usually as judgment.

> *Is a trumpet blown in a city, and the people are not afraid?*
> *Does disaster come to a city unless the LORD has done it?*
> (Amos 3:6, ESV)

Even in the early years of our own country, events were viewed and considered in light of the power and purpose of God. An early morning earthquake shook Boston in 1727. In his sermon titled, *The Terror of the Lord,* the Reverend Cotton Mather (1663-1728), wrote, "Let the natural causes of earthquakes be what the wise men of inquiry please; they and their causes are still under the government of Him that is the God of nature."

In our day, sadly, many in the church have become so affected by the world's way of thinking that we publically attribute these events to God at our own peril. Our culture has deteriorated to such a degree that the God of the Bible is hardly allowed into most Sunday sermons. Yet still, God reigns and all things do serve Him. We must see everything scripturally, including earthquakes, tornados, floods, and hurricanes, which are the more vocal messengers of the Lord. If God is sovereign, be assured that these events are not accidental or a "quirk of nature"; He is Creator, Sustainer, and Ruler over all things. Never be in doubt: ALL THINGS SERVE HIM!

> *Forever, O LORD, Your word,*
> *Is firmly fixed in the heavens.*
> *Your faithfulness endures to all generations,*
> *You have established the earth, and it stands fast.*
> *By Your appointment they stand this day,*
> *For all things are your servants.*
> (Psalm 119:89-91, ESV)

When God's children suffer, the first question should be: "Have I committed some sin which has brought this suffering upon me?"

(See James 5:15.) If the answer is "Yes," then confess, repent, and seek His mercy without delay. However dark the cloud of suffering, judgment for the Christian is temporal not eternal; He is near, full of pity, love, and power. He may withdraw from us and allow us to feel the serpent's bite, not to destroy us but to remind us of our misery and helplessness without Him. He knows us, loves us, and will not leave us to sin's destructive venom.

However, keep in mind that an unbeliever's suffering may be both temporal *and* eternal. He will definitely suffer under the consequences and penalty of sin. This book is not written to the unbeliever except as a warning and a plea: seek the Lord while He may be found, call upon Him while He is near.

Suffering May Be the Chastisement of the Lord
God disciplines His children; He chastens those He loves. Chastisement for the child of God is active proof of the love of God for us (Hebrews 12:5-11). Note particularly verse six: *"Those whom the Lord loves He disciplines."* This very thought is repeated in Revelation 3:19, *"Those whom I love, I reprove and discipline."* There is a great lesson here for parents of young children; discipline and chastisement are proofs of love.

God uses all kinds of methods to chastise and correct His children: a soft whisper, a gust of shame, weakness, sickness, and sometimes even death. All means are at His command. When some members of the Corinthian church were abusing the Lord's Table, Paul issued serious warnings:

> *Let a person examine himself, then, and so eat of the bread and drink of the cup. For anyone who eats and drinks without discerning the body eats and drinks judgment on himself. That is why many of you are weak and ill, and some have died. But if we judged*

> *ourselves truly, we would not be judged. But when we are judged by the Lord, we are disciplined so that we may not be condemned along with the world.* (1 Corinthians 11:28-32, ESV)

Discipline and chastisement from the Lord are always to correct, mature, or both. The same should be true when you discipline your children. Listen to these passages:

> *He who withholds his rod hates his son, but he who loves him disciplines him diligently...Foolishness is bound up in the heart of a child; The rod of discipline will remove it far from him...Do not hold back discipline from the child, Although you strike him with the rod, he will not die. You shall strike him with the rod And rescue his soul from Sheol (hell)...The rod and reproof give wisdom, But a child who gets his own way brings shame to his mother.* (Proverbs 13:24, 22:15, 23:13-14, 29:15)

As it is with a parent who loves his child, if you are Christ's, His love for you will be made known through His "weeding and cultivating" discipline. He is carrying out His kind intent and design for you. All has been done *"for those whom He foreknew He also predestined to become conformed to the image of His Son"* (Romans 8:29).

It's never His delight to have us suffer needlessly. All our medicines are carefully mixed and measured by the Great Physician and are exactly what we need. He knows our sickness, our mind, our flesh, our heart. Christ the Son drank the cup of Wrath; now we drink of the cup of our Father's Grace.

Suffering May Be an Assault of Satan
Luke records the healing of a woman who had been crippled for 18 long years. Jesus specifically says that she was one *"whom Satan has bound for eighteen long years..."* (Luke 13:16).

Paul wrote concerning Satan's attack on his body when he described his "thorn in the flesh." He specifically says that the agent of the thorn was *"a messenger of Satan..."* (2 Corinthians 12:7-10). Amazing passage! The Lord used Satan to accomplish His purpose by bringing Paul to total dependence on God.

Job's suffering came as direct assaults from Satan, who delights in causing suffering in the bodies, lives, and souls of God's people. But however fierce the beast and frightening his roar, he is on God's chain, and can go no further than the chain allows. Satan had no power over Job except as he was permitted by the Lord (Job 1-2). Remember also, Paul stated that his thorn was a "gift." Satan does not give gifts. The Lord Himself was the ultimate source of their pain, using Satan as the delivery instrument. He prowls and roars throughout the earth, and especially loves hunting the weak and wounded in DarkLand. But even in the darkest terrain, the promises of the King are posted and stepping stones are laid by Him to point the way of escape. Satan may bring suffering, but only by permission, and never without purpose: our good and God's glory.

Suffering May Come by Invitation
People often invite pain by recklessly engaging in activities known to have devastating consequences. In fact, there is a sense in which all suffering comes by choice—the choice of Adam in the Garden of Eden. He chose to disobey God. The invitation to know evil was delivered by Satan and the man accepted. Sin entered and the Creator's condemnation was instant. Genesis chapter three records the genesis of all suffering. To turn from that which is God's "good," is to take the invitation of evil. Evil always delivers its consequences.

Regardless of whether suffering, affliction, or pain come because of God's judgment, chastisement, Satan's assaults, or by our own bad choices, God's purpose for His child stands firm and will be accomplished (Romans 8:28). All things serve Him. The Christian will be conformed to the image of Christ, to the praise of the glory of His Name.

Answers may not come in ways that are expected, but God is not silent. He is not far away. Draw close to Him as a child to a loving Father. No good thing is withheld from God's elect. It is His promise.

Some Attitudes
Merely knowing the source and purpose for pain and suffering will not kill the anguish and hurting, but does help form and develop right attitudes while still in the dark times of life. I suspect that our attitude is more important than answers are in our ability to triumph. In most cases, our attitude toward our agonizing circumstances is a choice. Though we may never understand why life changed from laughter and sunshine to heartbreak and darkness, we can choose our response to it. This may be the struggle of a lifetime; I'm not saying it is easy; Trust me, I know. The right path is usually the most difficult. But we determine how pain and suffering will affect our lives by our attitudes, and our attitudes are the progeny of our thinking.

A young crippled student sold books during summer break to help pay his tuition. At one house the lady rudely turned him down. As he turned and walked away the woman realized that he was crippled. She called him back. "I didn't know you were crippled, I will buy a book from you!" she said. But the young man was not selling sympathy, he was selling books and he made sure she knew it. The woman asked, "Doesn't being a cripple color your life?" He replied, "Yes, but thank God I can choose the color." Pain and suffering do color our lives, but we can choose the color.

There are many responses to adversity, affliction, and suffering. People react and manage in different ways; for the Christian it must be by thinking and acting scripturally in the power of the Holy Spirit. God gives us the map and the power to walk the right path. Submit to Him; follow whatever light He gives and walk straight in it.

> He will not leave you to sink. He has appointed seasons of refreshment, and you shall find He does not forget you. Above all, keep close to the throne of grace. If we seem to get no good by attempting to draw near Him we may be sure we shall get none by keeping away from Him. [4]

Our own reasoning and instincts will ultimately work against us, and not for our good. Who you trust and follow in the midst of life's darkness and storms will determine whether you remain in the dark or prevail over it. Beware of the pits and blind paths that human reasoning and human nature point the suffering one toward. Here are three Attitudes that must be avoided; the Scriptures post warning signs so that we turn away from these paths and snares. Bitterness. Self-pity. Resignation.

Bitterness
Bitterness is seething anger, skepticism, and doubt: "God did this to me!"

"You could change this Lord! Why haven't You???"

Bitterness accuses and mistrusts God. Bitterness wraps its long strangling roots around the heart and sprouts poisonous weeds of selfish desires and resentment.

Bitterness is a tragic response to pain and suffering, giving to neither life nor affliction any meaning or purpose or remedy. Bitterness never takes away pain; it makes the people who are absorbed by it sullen, unpleasant, judgmental, and acid to the people in their lives.

If sorrow and suffering clamor for an explanation from God, should blessing also demand His explanations? Should the mysterious fires of affliction call into question the goodness of our sovereign God? If so, the justice of His many mysterious mercies and rivers of grace must also be called into the courtroom of our opinions. We should try to be consistent; if we mistrust in the bitter, we should also mistrust in the sweet.

Don't waste your life in bitterness. It accomplishes nothing good and exacts a heavy toll on the mind and body. You have to work at being bitter. The writer of Hebrews issues this warning: *"See to it that no one comes short of the grace of God; that no root of bitterness springing up causes trouble, and by it many be defiled"* (Hebrews 12:15).

Bitterness defiles you and it defiles others. Its offspring are vipers: anger, hate, wrath, slander, malice, jealousy, and on and on... You accommodate and nurture bitterness at your own peril; it carries within it *bitter* consequences.

> *You shall not hate your fellow countryman in your heart; you may surely reprove your neighbor, but shall not incur sins because of him. You shall not take vengeance, nor bear any grudge against the sons of your people, but you shall love your neighbor as yourself; I am the Lord.* (Leviticus 19:17-18)

Self-Pity
Self-pity is a defeatist attitude. The "Why Me?—I don't deserve this!" attitude is brother to self-righteousness and self-worship. Indulging self-pity is a step into the deeper bog of bitterness.

Too many people have overcome tremendous afflictions leaving for us great examples of courage and perseverance over huge difficulties. Beethoven was deaf, John Milton was blind, Robert Louis Stevenson had tuberculosis, Thomas Edison was nearly deaf, Lewis Braille was blinded at age three, Fanny Crosby was blinded when six months of age. All these, and countless others, overcame their infirmities and left behind patterns of perseverance and achievement. Adversity for them was only an experience in life—it was not the final act.

Self-pity is a miserable existence. It will flatter, isolate, and trap. Early on, it may be snug and cozy like a feather pillow, but with time it hardens and gives no rest. "Self-pity will parch your attitude, it will paralyze your abilities, and it will put off your achievements. It prohibits excellence and prevents expansion." I don't know who made that statement, but it's true.

Sinful Resignation
Demanding a full explanation from the Lord for what He has done is the height of intellectual pride. Yet no Christian should lie down during adversity with the attitude of "Well, whatever will be, will be!" No questions—no seeking understanding—total surrender to defeat by difficult circumstances. Certainly we should submit to the will and purpose of the Lord, but an attitude of resignation (I'll just grit my teeth, grin, and bear it) is more in the category of fatalism than submissiveness. Although an answer may not come immediately, it is not wrong to ask God why things happen. He is causing all things to work together for good for you; seek to comprehend in order to mature and marvel at His wisdom and power. He gave you a mind; use it. Habakkuk did. He asked, *"Why do You make me see iniquity, and cause me to look on wickedness?"* (Habakkuk 1:3).

The childlike attitude of a trusting heart during the darkest times is honoring to Him who loves us so much. A humble quest for understanding is never crushed when clothed with a right motive. To have total comprehension of all that God is doing in times of pain and adversity in our life will never happen. Don't assume that you could understand all God's plans, purposes, and providence even if He told you every detail. Our mental capacity may be a little lacking when it comes to grasping the full picture of God's marvelous providence and purpose.

> *"My thoughts are not your thoughts, nor are your ways My ways," declares the Lord. "For as the heavens are higher than the earth, so are My ways higher than your ways, and My thoughts than your thoughts."* (Isaiah 55:8-9)

> *Oh, the depth of the riches both of the wisdom and knowledge of God! How unsearchable are His judgments and unfathomable His ways!* (Romans 11:33)

God does nothing without purpose. His intentions and works are carried out in love and under His divine management. He never gets distracted; He never forgets His business. At times we must be content with a partial understanding until we get to heaven. Paul wrote, *"now we see in a mirror dimly, but then face to face; now I know in part, but then I will know fully just as I also have been fully known"* (1 Corinthians 13:12). So, as we acknowledge that there are some things we can understand and there are some things we will not fully understand while on this earth, we must trust the Lord. Faith is not blind, it has the greatest object: Christ our King. Don't lie down in a sleep of fatalistic misery and miss the treasure to be gathered.

Bitterness and self-pity can destroy us. Unquestioned resignation (fatalism) or demanding total understanding can never help or give any relief to a life in pain. Godly perseverance works by faith; faith in Him who deserves that trust and can deliver on His promises. Trust Him and you will trust Him more. Even when you think God is doing nothing, He is doing everything.

> *Who is among you that fears the LORD,*
> *That obeys the voice of His servant,*
> *That walks in darkness and has no light?*
> *Let him trust in the name of the LORD and rely on his God.*
> (Isaiah 50:10)

Some Results of Pain and Suffering
We must search out and rest upon what the Bible teaches in regard to pain and suffering. Blessing and maturing are bound up in the fabric of our afflictions. It is not God's primary purpose that we always enjoy lives of physical ease. Were He to indulge and coddle his children by endless happiness and smooth paths, we would be the poorest and dimmest of lights in this world. Our spiritual muscles would be weak and vulnerable, and our knowledge of Him just a shadow.

We are soldiers all, and will be trained and taught in the school of the cross until we are made into the image of our Captain. Adversity and affliction are teachers in that school. If the Lord Jesus was made perfect through suffering (Hebrews 2:10), surely we should not complain when He leads us through the Refiner's fire also.

When we ponder and meditate on the Scriptures, we discover jewels of blessing associated with suffering. Consider these: Patience, Humility, Obedience, Sympathy, Inspiration, Glory.

Patience
The purpose of God is not to always exempt us from difficulty, but to produce in us a Godly character—a character that will respond to life's sorrows and darkest hours with patience, and to strengthen us to bear them. Pain and Suffering are God's messengers and trainers,

and patience is one of their specialties. He gives us a cup of affliction, but it is mixed throughout with mercies; in the end it will prove to be the medicine most needed. In the Bible the words *endurance, perseverance,* and *patience* are often translated from the same root word. *"Knowing that the testing of our faith produces endurance"* (James 1:3). Paul wrote, *"knowing that tribulation brings about perseverance"* (Romans 5:3b).

There is an old adage that says, "No sailor ever distinguished himself on a smooth sea." Almost anything worthwhile requires some struggle or even pain. Strength isn't built by lifting feathers.

Humility
Humility is another of those spiritual jewels that comes wrapped in the package of pain and suffering. It seems that suffering has a way of knocking pride, arrogance, and nonsense out of us. Failure, pain, and suffering acquaint us with our own weaknesses and point us to His great power. Instructing the Corinthian church Paul wrote, *"Indeed, we had the sentence of death within ourselves so that we would not trust in ourselves, but in God who raises the dead"* (2 Corinthians 1:9). Anything that reveals our own inadequacy and God's all-sufficiency in Christ is a blessing. To see God as He really is and ourselves as we really are is one of the most precious results of affliction and adversity when the Christian responds scripturally. Pride and self-dependence have to be driven out of the heart and exposed for the empty boasters that they are. Humility bows low before God knowing that He will do all and supply all that is needed. Whatever circumstance comes our way is just what we need—no more, no less. We cannot ultimately fail as long as He keeps His word. Humility rests in that fact.

Obedience
As the psalmist David wrote, *"Before I was afflicted I went astray, but now I keep Your word…It is good for me that I was afflicted that*

I may learn your statutes" (Psalm 119:67, 71). Affliction in the Christian's life brings about a desire to repent, obey, and long for God's presence. The Bible is saturated with this truth. When we are put in circumstances of darkness and hurt, it *becomes* the Christian's response to look to the Word of God and seek His face and pleasure. "What do you want me to do Lord? How must I respond to please You?"

There is a rather sobering verse of Scripture in the Book of Hebrews which speaks of Christ and it reads, *"Although He was a Son, He learned obedience from the things which He suffered"* (Hebrews 5:8). If the Lord who was the perfect Lamb of God had to learn obedience through suffering, how much more necessary is suffering for you and me in order for us to learn obedience? We often see this principle in children. In many cases it matters not how many times or how often parents tell children the danger of a particular thing, most children only learn that truth when they disobey and suffer the consequences.

Sympathy
Sympathy is another of the by-products of afflictions. The most tenderhearted among men will be those who have suffered most. Hardship mellows us and makes us more understanding and compassionate with others who are suffering.

> *Blessed be the God and Father of our Lord Jesus Christ, the Father of mercies and God of all comfort, who comforts us in all our afflictions so that we will be able to comfort those who are in any affliction with the comfort with which we ourselves are comforted by God.* (2 Corinthians 1:3-4)

Suffering fashions us into true comforters of others. When I was in the hospital after having heart surgery, a doctor related to me that he once worked with a heart surgeon who would not prescribe pain medication to his patients after performing open heart surgery on them. He didn't think his patients needed the medication, *until* he himself had to have open heart surgery. Through his own experience of pain, he learned the necessity for pain medication. The most comforting surgeon is the one who has had surgery himself. The person best equipped to comfort others is the person who has been comforted through their own suffering. Your afflictions in the depths of DarkLand just might be the Lord preparing you to be the comforter of some loved one or fellow Christian who will soon be in the pits and darkness of suffering. In this case would you not agree that your suffering would be for good?

Inspiration
Our suffering can inspire others. As we grow in faith, patience, obedience, and sympathy through suffering, others are encouraged and inspired. Being a pastor for many years, I have seen many people suffer. The most inspiring were those who suffered without complaining, blaming others, or becoming angry with the Lord; they held fast their faith in Him and praised His goodness even in the midst of their hurting and pain. The way we handle suffering is a sermon to all observers. The question we should ask is, "When I suffer am I a comfort to others or am I a grief or stumbling block?"

When Henry Drummond died, D.L. Moody said, "The homecoming of Drummond adds one more attraction to heaven." That statement was encouragement to those who mourned his death. The loss of a loved one who knows the Lord often makes others homesick for heaven. A life of ease and a smooth path never produces the precious traits and character that can empathize, console, and inspire. Furthermore, the world sees how we react in adversity; the world sees proof of the power and reality of God in the dark seasons of the Christian's walk.

Suffering Glorifies the Lord
Paul rejoiced while in a Roman prison. He gave thanks for the thorn in his flesh (2 Corinthians 12:9-10). Suffering provides the Christian an opportunity to glorify his Savior by patient obedience. By seeing affliction and adversity as instruments of the Lord, our attitude will be a display of praise and thanksgiving. In that attitude the Lord will be glorified.

For a while when I was young, my father was a furniture salesman. He told me a story about attending a sales meeting at a furniture factory. At that meeting it was demonstrated that the best oak furniture was cut from trees that grew in areas where there were lots of wind and storms. The storms and the winds caused the trees to twist and sway making the grain of the wood to be much more tightly knit than other wood. This stressed and battered wood made the most beautiful furniture. The storms, afflictions, and times of darkness in life are the agents which the Lord uses to make us useful and beautiful. The winds and storms of adversity and pain form within us patience, humility, obedience, sympathy, and inspiration.

As we are sculpted and refined into the image of Christ, we begin to reflect Him like the moon reflects the light of the sun. He melts us, molds us, and polishes us—all to bring glory to Himself. What a great privilege for us.

> Once I heard a song of sweetness
> As it cleft the morning air,
> Sounding in its blest completeness,
> Like a tender pleading prayer;
> And I sought to find the singer,
> Whence the wondrous song was born,
> And I found a bird, sore wounded,
> Pinioned [disabled] by an ugly thorn.

I have seen a soul of sadness
While its wings with pain were furled,
Giving hope and cheer and gladness
That should bless a weeping world;
And I knew that life of sweetness,
 Was of pain and sorrow born,
And a stricken soul was singing
With its heart against a thorn.

Ye are told of One who loves you,
 Of a Saviour crucified,
Ye are told of nails that pinioned,
And a spear that pierced His side;
Ye are told of cruel scourging,
 Of a Saviour bearing scorn,
And He died for our salvation,
With His brow against a thorn.

Ye are not above the Master!
Will you breathe a sweet refrain?
And His grace will be sufficient,
When your heart is pierced with pain;
Will you live to bless His loved one,
Tho' your life be bruised and torn,
Like a bird that sang so sweetly
With its heart against a thorn? [5]

---

1 Martin Luther, quoted by A.W. Pink in *Gleanings from Paul*
2 Charles Spurgeon, christian-quotes.ochristian.com
3 C.S. Lewis, quoted by George Horsington in an article titled *Ship Management*, 2004. The author is a ship manager based in the former Soviet Union.
4 John Newton, *Cardiphonia*, Morgan and Scott LD, 1911, p. 344
5 Author Unknown

4

STRESS

We are not necessarily doubting that God will do the best for us; we are wondering how painful the best will turn out to be. [1]

Without the emotions of love, joy, peace, discouragement, stress, fear, anger, disappointment, faith, and expectation man would be no more than a sophisticated biological computer and probably on sale in any computer store. The Psalmist said that we are "fearfully and wonderfully made" (Psalm 139:14).

Let me say at the outset that when considering all the difficulties and pressures in the world cultures of our time, no person who is not a committed Christian has the ability within themselves to successfully handle the stressful events and temptations which press in from every direction. If men could effectively handle stress without a close walk with the Lord, they wouldn't become debilitatingly stressed; no one enjoys the mental and physical draining state which unrelenting stress brings.

Stress is commonly experienced and greatly discussed, and it should be because the Bible says a great deal about "worry" (stress). The prophet Habakkuk was stressed as he waited for his enemies to attack.

> *I heard and my inward parts trembled, at the sound my lips quivered. Decay enters my bones, and in my place I tremble. Because I must wait quietly for the day of distress, for the people to arise who will invade us.* (Habakkuk 3:16)

Anxiety in a man's heart weighs it down,
But a good word makes it glad
(Proverbs 12:25)

Jesus warned that the worry of the world would choke out the word of God from the heart of a man, *"and the worry of the world and the deceitfulness of wealth choke the word, and it becomes unfruitful"* (Matthew 13:22). Worry, stress, and anxiety have consequences.

However, there is a *Profitable Kind of Stress* that is not riddled with worry; all stress is not bad. In fact, you cannot live successfully without some stress. There's a certain type of stress that gives us alertness and focus. The teacher as well as the student is under a certain amount of stress: the teacher, to communicate; the student, to learn and understand. The airline pilot as well as the passenger is under a certain kind of stress. I, the passenger, am praying that the pilot is under some stress to get that big bird off the ground and land it safely when we get to our destination. The same is true with the doctor, athlete, lawyer, pastor, executive, and yes, even parents and children—all are under stress. While I write this chapter, I experience a certain kind of stress trying to communicate with you, the reader. At the same time you experience a kind of stress as you read, seeking to comprehend and understand. Certainly, we would not say that this kind of stress is bad, for it sharpens and focuses our mind and body.

Guilt is an example of a good and God-given kind of stress. Guilt is like the warning lights on the dashboard of your car. When one of those warning lights appears, you have two choices. You can ignore it and drive on until your engine blows up, or you can get to a mechanic and get the problem fixed. Guilt flashes inside us; you can find out what the sin is that is causing it, repent of it, and receive forgiveness, or you can ignore it and end up suffering severe stress, discouragement, even depression, and perhaps physical illness.

Stress is involved with most everything in life. The singer stresses the vocal cords to reach the right pitch. Strings on musical instruments like the guitar, piano, banjo, harp, and violin are stressed to produce beautiful music. The soldier on the battlefield is under stress to protect himself and his buddies. When you drive down the road, you are under stress, or you should be, for it enhances alertness. No part of life is completely exempt from stress in some form and degree. Everyone has their share of both good and bad stress; it's a part of the fabric of life. Therefore guard against thinking that all stress is bad.

Problems occur when stress becomes uncontrolled; when stress controls us. Constant and unrelenting stress is a tormentor physically, emotionally, and spiritually. Good stress focuses the mind to act rightly like a shepherd leading sheep; bad stress controls, commands, and drives the mind like a butcher goading and shoving the sheep to their destruction.

Doctors tell us that stress is a great contributor to myriads of physical and emotional aliments among which are colitis, ulcers, hypertension, cancer, upset stomach, headaches, allergies, skin disorders, heart disease, arthritis, rheumatism, even insanity. We may be living in the most stressful society that has ever existed. It's said that life in our present culture can be best described with three words, HURRY, WORRY, AND BURY!

Of the ten leading causes of death in America today, eight are stress related. It has been predicted that the average business executive has a one in three chance of dying from a heart attack by age sixty due to stress.

But be alert to the disguises of sin; sometimes stress is used as an excuse for not doing the things which should be done. We often hear the excuse, "I'm stressed out and not thinking right," or "I'm too stressed to sit down and read to my little girl. She just needs to go to bed!" The examples are endless. In these cases stress probably is not the problem. Maybe sin or maybe laziness would better define this kind of mind-set. What then is stress? According to Dr. Brian Griggs, a physician: "Stress is the body's response to any demand placed on it in which the body prepares to meet a threatening situation. In all such situations the body gets ready for flight or fight. Blood pressure increases, adrenalin shoots to the extremities, digestion slows, muscles tense." He further stated that "life in the past 25 years has become so hectic that our bodies are in stressful states most of the time." [2]

Bad stress comes from wrong reactions to circumstances, creating such an intense pressure on the body and emotions that one is overwhelmed under the load. Here are a few examples of Stress Triggers:

> Sustained conflicts in relationships in family, on the job, in school, etc.
> Taking on responsibilities that are not yours
> Overloaded schedule when there is not time taken to relax
> Feeling inadequate or unqualified to perform a particular function assigned to you; this can be particularly true in a church setting
> Trying to live up to standards others set for you that may or may not be right standards

How can a person know when they are stressed to the point of being overwhelmed? Here are some symptoms of Overload Stress:

Sad or feeling depressed
Stomach disorders, headaches, and sometimes chest pains
Feeling that you are constantly under pressure or being hurried
Attacks of anxiety
Overindulging in alcohol, chain smoking, overeating, and taking drugs
Sleeping disorders
Allergic reactions—asthma, eczema, hives
Using words in sinful cutting ways

One of the difficulties in dealing with stress is that everyone's experiences with stress are different and not everyone reacts to stress the same way. There are lots of detour signs along the path of life pointing to bypass roads that promise relief from stress and their seductiveness can be very strong—drugs, alcohol, pleasures, sports, work—and millions of people go down those roads. Others internalize—holding it in—keeping it inside and to themselves, often developing into physical problems. Others deal with it in an external way by lashing out in anger and sarcasm. Any one of these ways of handling stress is sinful and compounds the problem. Since each of us will face many stressful situations in life, we *must* learn how to manage those situations rightly, and the clue to doing that is outlined for us in the Word of God. We must think scripturally as we walk past the snares and traps alongside our path in life so as not to plunge onto a wrong trail that leads into the shadow, darkness and despair of DarkLand.

When stress comes in the "monster" form, how do we deal biblically with this brutish ogre? The enemies of the Christian can be defeated and victory can be secured. A good starting place is to look at the life of our Lord. He was constantly under pressures, but there were no signs of stress. There were overwhelming demands on His time; He seldom had privacy; He was constantly interrupted; He was misunderstood, criticized, and ridiculed, but He remained at peace under all these pressures. How did He face these problems; the very problems which cause us to get "stressed"? I want to show you at least seven principles you can use to deal with stress as observed in the life of Christ our Lord.

Identification: Know Who You Are
Many years ago, there was a young couple in a church where I was pastor. They had two children, but one day the husband and father left, leaving only a note for his young wife and little family which read something to the effect, "I'm going to find myself." This may sound strange, but sadly it's not an uncommon expression. People who are constantly searching for identity in some feeling or accomplishment often say "I'm trying to find out who I am." Some folks search for identity in sports, business, entertainment, possessions, power, or try to mask their desire for significance with alcohol, drugs, or sex. Certainly this is not uncommon for a person who does not have a saving relationship with the Lord Jesus Christ, or even people who are true Christians but are very immature in the faith. And yes, *many* try to find identity in religious busyness.

Did Jesus have this problem? Not at all. He knew who He was. He said, *"I am the bread of life...the good shepherd...the resurrection...the way...the truth...the life...the vine ... I and the Father are one, when you have seen Me you see the Father also."* Because He knew who He was and His purpose for being here, He had no problem dealing with the pressures of life. He reacted rightly in every situation.

The only true identity you will ever have is in a saving relationship with Him. We are who God says we are. We hear and read so much about self-worth and good self-image, but there's no such thing as a good self-image except when we are united to the Lord Jesus Christ through saving and sustaining faith. Man lost his identity—his good self-image in the Garden of Eden when our first parents fell into sin and plunged the whole of the human race into sin and condemnation, *"Just as through one man (Adam) sin entered into the world, and death through sin, and so death spread to all men, because all sinned"* (Romans 5:12).

When Adam, the Federal head of the human race, disobeyed God, he fell from his created nature; he lost all his original created righteousness which allowed him to enjoy fellowship with God. Adam became unable to do what God had created him to do, namely, glorify his Creator. As a consequence, man in his sinful state is incomplete, unhappy, without peace in his very being. He is separated from God and incapable of doing what God commands; man lost his identity. Is it any wonder that unbelievers are stressed? They have lost their identity, and are searching for it in countless empty ways.

> William Law said, "If you have not chosen the Kingdom of God, it will make in the end no difference what you have chosen instead." Those are hard words to take. Will it really make no difference whether it was women or patriotism, cocaine or art, whisky or a seat in the Cabinet, money or science? Well, surely no difference that matters. We shall have missed the end for which we are formed and rejected the only thing that satisfies. Does it matter to a man dying in a desert, by which choice of route he missed the only well? [3]

Only *in Christ* is there any real and true identity. He puts His stamp and seal on us; we are His, purchased and loved.

This first principle in handling stress as a Christian is to reaffirm your relationship with Christ. I cannot say it too much: only *in Christ* is true identity found. Only at the Cross will the sinner learn his true identity: condemned and alienated from God. Only at the

Cross does the Christian see his true identity: a sinner forgiven, sin debt paid, reconciled to God, and made an heir of salvation, eternal life with glory crowned. At the Cross and in Christ you will know who you are—a child of God.

If you don't know who you are, be assured, someone else will be telling you who they think you are, and you'll begin to believe them. If others dictate your identity, manipulation usually follows, along with pressure to be something you're not. That is STRESS!

So if you want to apply this principle of knowing who you truly are—first know *whose* you are. If you are not a Christian, you are a creature God has created and placed here on this earth to glorify Him. Therefore, by creation you belong to Him—your Creator. Recognizing this is a good *starting place* for the unbeliever to come to a saving relationship with Jesus Christ. If you are a Christian, you should know that you belong to Him in several ways. You were created by God, given to His Son, bought with the precious blood of His Son, and birthed into the family of God by His Holy Spirit. This means that you are not your own. If you are the beloved of Christ, you are loved, you are provided for, and you have a purpose in life. That all-important purpose is to glorify your Savior. Settling in your mind "who you are" and "whose you are" is a stress reliever. Knowing who you are gives you genuine purpose in life—God's purpose.

> God sought thee wandering, set thee right;
> Turned thy darkness into light. [4]

Dedication: Know Who You Are To Please
Christ said, "*I can do nothing on My own initiative. As I hear, I judge; and My judgment is just, because I do not seek My own will, but the will of Him who sent Me*" (John 5:30). The issue was settled with Jesus. He knew whose will He was seeking to please and it

mattered not what others thought He should do. He wasn't trying to please everyone. His mission was to do the will of His Father.

When you know who it is you are to please and resolve to live at His command, you won't be pulled in countless directions trying to please everyone. Even the Lord Jesus cannot please everyone and He doesn't try. If you try to satisfy everyone, you will be severely pressured and tempted in three areas.

> You will be worried about *criticism*—what others think of you.
> You will be worried about *competition*—afraid others are getting more than you.
> You will be worried about *conflicts*—feel threatened when someone disagrees with you.

Your life is in some ways like a train. A train is built to run on tracks. As long as it runs on tracks it runs freely and smoothly. But if it jumps the tracks, it becomes nothing but a pile of metal useful for nothing until put back on the tracks. Man was created to glorify God, but in Adam we jumped track; Adam's descendants now come into this world off the tracks. David said, *"The wicked are estranged from the womb; they go astray from birth, speaking lies"* (Psalm 58:3-4, ESV). By the grace and power of God, the Christian has been put back on the tracks through the regenerating work of the Holy Spirit. As long as his eyes are fixed on Christ and his focus is to glorify God, he will handle the pressures of life rightly. But if he glances away and forgets his goal, stress and doubt will hunt him down because he has, to some degree, jumped the tracks. It's a stressful situation for a man to be off the tracks, for it is to be in DarkLand where thinking and actions are probably only reactions to the rocky bumpy terrain. Stay on the track even if it goes through a dark tunnel.

Sit down and meditate on whose will it is you are trying to please. If it's your own, you're under stress; if it's the will of someone else, you're stressed. The only 'will' you should be seeking to please is the Lord's will. He saved you for that very purpose. Only in seeking to be useful and pleasing to Him will you be relieved from the destructive stresses in this world. You belong to the King; stay on the King's Highway; the King is your loving Savior, Jesus Christ.

Remember *Who* you are! Remember *Whose* you are!

> Now may the Lord reveal His face,
> And teach our stammering tongues
> To make His sovereign, reigning grace
> The subject of our songs.
>
> No sweeter subject can invite
> A sinner's heart to sing,
> Or more display the glorious right
> Of our exalted King.
>
> Grace reigns to pardon crimson sins,
> To melt the hardest hearts;
> And from the work it once begins
> It never once departs.
>
> 'Twas grace that called our souls at first;
> By grace thus far we're come;
> And grace will help us through the worst,
> And lead us safely home. [5]

Organization: Know What You Are Trying To Accomplish
As a general rule people who are constantly "stressed out" are unorganized. They have no plans or goals for their lives and are prone to dream about what should be or what could be, rather than doing it.

Jesus was very organized. He said, *"Even if I bear witness of myself, my witness is true for I know where I came from and where I am going"* (John 8:14). Jesus knew who He was, where He came from, why He was here, where He was going, and how to get there. That's organization! Consequently, He had no stress. Pressures yes, but stressed out—NO!

Further, He taught *us* how to live a life free of sinful stress. Read carefully what He said in Matthew 6:25-33 concerning worry and trust. In this passage the Lord displays His great wisdom and compassion, being well aware of the difficulties and concerns we meet with in a sinful fallen world. He understands our responsibilities to provide for our families and the difficulties we face in fulfilling those responsibilities. So He gives us training and encouragement.

He instructs us *"do not be worried about your life, as to what you will eat or what you will drink; nor for your body; as to what you will put on. Is not life more than food, and the body more than clothing"* (Matthew 6:25). Here He speaks to the basic essentials of life in this world: food, drink, and clothing.

Then He reminds us of God's providential care of His creation. His instructions and encouragements are simple. If God feeds the birds of the air, if He clothes the lilies of the field with beauty, if He clothes the grass of the field, then why should you be stressed or worried, *"will He not much more clothe you"* (Matthew 6:30)? You are of more worth than the birds, lilies, and grass. You were created in His image. He redeemed you with His own blood. He indwells you with the Holy Spirit. He didn't do this for the birds, lilies, or grass.

He adds to all this a soul-searching question, *"And who of you by being worried can add a single hour to his life"* (Matthew 6:27). In other words, what can worry accomplish? The question is its own answer: worry accomplishes nothing. Christ our King then instructs us not to worry about tomorrow, *"So do not worry about tomorrow; for tomorrow will care for itself. Each day has enough trouble of its own"* (Matthew 6:34).

Worry in the Christian demonstrates a lack of faith and an ungrateful spirit *"But if God so clothed the grass of the field, which today is alive and tomorrow is thrown into the oven, will He not much more clothe you, O you of little faith"* (Matthew 6:30). We are not content when we are worried and stressed about the things of this world.

> He that has made my heaven secure
> Will here all good provide;
> While Christ is rich I can't be poor;
> What can I want beside? [6]

Then Jesus hands us the *key* that locks stress and worry out: *"...your heavenly Father knows that you need all these things. But seek first His kingdom and His righteousness, and all these things will be added to you"* (Matthew 6:32-33). It's the key to organization and priority setting. Remember this, unless you make plans, and set goals and priorities for your life, others will set them for you. You'll live trying to meet the world's standard for success: that spells STRESS. Every day you live by one of two things: *priorities* or *pressures*. You either set priorities or you will live under the pressures of what others think you should be and do.

Jesus has set the priority for us, *"seek first the kingdom of God and His righteousness..."* (KJV). That righteousness can only be found in a saving relationship with Christ. Everything should be viewed and prioritized as service to the King. The Apostle Paul expressed this priority for his life:

> *But whatever things were gain to me, those things I have counted as loss for the sake of Christ. More than that I count all things to be loss in view of the surpassing value of knowing Christ Jesus my Lord, for whom I have suffered the loss of all things, and count them but rubbish so that I may gain Christ, and may be found in Him, not having a righteousness of my own derived from the Law, but that which is through faith in Christ, the righteousness which comes from God on the basis of faith, that I may know Him and the power of His resurrection and the fellowship of His sufferings, being conformed to His death; in order that I may attain to the resurrection from the dead.* (Philippians 3:7-11)

Concentration: Focus on One Thing at a Time
Don't allow yourself to be sidetracked from seeking the kingdom of God and His righteousness; He must always be First; Christ never comes next. Jesus refused to be sidetracked. In Galilee He performed many miracles and cast out demons; crowds of people came to Him and brought their sick, and He healed them. The next day He left and went to a secluded place, but the crowds searched for Him trying to keep Him from leaving them (see Luke 4:43). Jesus said to them, *"I must preach the kingdom of God to the other cities also, for I was sent for this purpose."* He refused to be diverted from His mission.

Jesus was never distracted, never side-tracked, and always concentrated on His mission. He had a clear priority and He never veered from the path required to complete it. When you determine in your heart and mind to do right, you'll find many people who want to redirect your efforts. Don't allow people to pressure and divert you from your purpose and priorities. Some of Satan's most effective diversionary tools are involvement in what people label as "good things," but which distract and side-track from God's "best things."

It's so easy for us to do good things, not necessarily because of dedication or consecration to the cause of Christ, but because of pride. In the year 1714 Bernard Mandeville (1670-1733) wrote, "Pride and vanity have built more hospitals than all the virtues together." It's amazing what pride can accomplish. Men finance and construct magnificent buildings in order to get their name inscribed on them. Pride will give time and money to good causes, not necessarily out of a heart of commitment to the cause, but because of the recognition it brings. Certainly the Lord can use these works in spite of the motives involved, but let's not label it "serving the Lord."

In writing to the church at Colossae, Paul said, *"Therefore if you have been raised up with Christ, keep seeking the things above, where Christ is, seated at the right hand of God. Set your mind on the things above, not on the things that are on earth. For you have died and your life is hidden with Christ in God"* (Colossians 3:1-3). Make this your focus; concentrate on Him and His priorities and stress will diminish greatly.

Meditation: Form a Habit (Not a Ritual) of Prayer
The word "habit" has several meanings and connotations, but I am referring to the *practice* of praying in a planned and persistent manner; it's the opposite of praying periodically, haphazardly, and without purpose, or regarding prayer as merely a "911" to use when we're in trouble. Jesus practiced prayer in a systematic way: *"But Jesus Himself would often slip away to the wilderness and pray"* (Luke 6:16). Over and over you read of Jesus going off by Himself to pray. In Mark 1:35 we read, *"In the early morning, while it was still dark, Jesus got up, left the house, and went away to a secluded place, and was praying there."* This was His habit, His practice.

There's an old saying that goes like this: "Nothing is ever settled till it is settled right, and nothing is ever settled right till it is settled with

God." If this statement is true (I believe it is), then no one who is stressed will ever be free from that burden until time is spent in prayer with the Lord. If you examine the Scriptures carefully you will find that our Lord did not make any decisions without first spending time in prayer. How many professing Christians head out in the morning to face a cruel ruthless world without praying for God to give strength and wisdom to face the issues of the day? Those same people probably wonder why they're always so stressed out.

> Of all things, guard against neglecting
> God in the secret place of prayer. [7]

On May 19, 1872, Charles Spurgeon said the following in his Sunday morning sermon, *Golden Vials Full of Odours*, at the Metropolitan Tabernacle in London:

> The more we pray, the more we want to pray. The more we pray, the more we can pray. The more we pray, the more we shall pray. He who prays little will pray less, but he who prays much will pray more. And he who prays more, will desire to pray more abundantly. Prayer and meditation are indispensable to the Christian if he would have control of stress in his life.

One characteristic of fallen man is that when he loses his way, he doubles his pace. Countless people are that way: speeding through life full of worry and stress with no idea of where to find relief. Instead of following the Light that shines in the darkness, they stare at the darkness and grope. Jesus said, *"Come to Me, all who are weary and heavy-laden, and I will give you rest"* (Matthew 11:28).

> Does the Gospel word proclaim
> Rest for those who weary be?

> Then, my soul, put in thy claim;
> Sure that promise speaks to thee. [8]

Recreation: Take Time Off to Rest
Jesus sent the twelve out on a preaching mission. Upon their return they reported to Him all that had happened. He said to them, *"Come away by yourselves to a secluded place and rest a while"* (Mark 6:31). The disciples were obviously tired and stressed. As already pointed out, Jesus Himself often went either to the mountains or the desert for rest and prayer.

Have you thought about the fact that one of the Commandments has to do with rest? The Sabbath was made for man, not man for the Sabbath. God intends for you to rest. The Sabbath was given to man for a day of rest and worship. If you don't take time for rest, you'll soon feel the pressure of life overwhelming you; you'll be stressed to the limit. I once heard the old Baptist preacher, Vance Havner, say, "If you don't come apart, you'll come apart."

God even instructed Israel to give the land rest every seven years, *"You shall sow your land for six years and gather in its yield, but on the seventh year you shall let it rest and lie fallow..."* (Exodus 23:10-11). So even the land gets stressed and needs rest and recovery. Getting alone with the Lord for rest and prayer can do wonders for a tired soul.

Transformation: Give Your Stress to Christ
This one Jesus did not need since He is God in the Flesh. As the God-man, He takes our stress upon Himself. He invites us to come to Him and He will give us rest (Matthew 11:28-30). The Apostle Peter wrote, *"...humble yourselves under the mighty hand of God, that He may exalt you at the proper time, casting all your anxiety (stress) on Him, because He cares for you"* (1 Peter 5:6-7). "When a

man is anxious—he cannot pray with faith, or serve his Master. When you worry and fret about your lot and circumstances, you are meddling with Christ's business, and neglecting your own! You have been attempting the *providing* work—and forgetting that it is yours to obey. Be wise and attend to the *obeying*—and let Christ manage the *providing*." [9]

Study the following passages carefully and you will find promise and encouragement in dealing with the struggles in your life.

Psalm 37:1-7	Isaiah 43:107
Psalm 34	Isaiah 16:3
Psalm 4:8	Proverbs 15:15
Psalm 121	Matthew 6:25-34
Psalm 23	Romans 5:1
John 16:33	Philippians 4:4-9

I compare the troubles which we have to undergo in the course of the year—to a great bundle of sticks, far too large for us to lift. But God does not require us to carry the whole bundle at once. He mercifully unties the bundle, and gives us first one stick, which we are to carry today; and then another, which we carry tomorrow, and so forth.

We can easily manage our trouble, if we would only carry the trouble appointed for each day. But the load will be too heavy for us if we carry yesterday's burden over again today, and then add the burden of tomorrow to the weight, before we are required to bear it. [10]

1   C.S. Lewis, *Letters of C.S. Lewis*, April 29, 1957, Paragraph 1, p. 285
2   Quoted by Jan Markell, *Overcoming Stress*, Victor Books, 1982, p. 8
3   C.S. Lewis, *The Weight of Glory*, "A Slip of the Tongue" (first published 1963), Paragraph 11, p. 131
4   William Cowper, *Olney Hymnal*, Book I, #118
5   John Newton, *Olney Hymnal*, Book III
6   John Ryland, Jr., *Gadsby Hymnal*, Part 1, #247
7   William Wilberforce, thinkexist.com/quotes/william_wilberforce
8   John Newton, *Olney Hymnal*, Book III, #14
9   Charles Haddon Spurgeon, *Morning and Evening: Complete and Unabridged*, Hendrickson Publishing, 2010, Morning of December 19
10 John Newton, *Out of the Depths*, Moody Press, p. 159

5

FAILURE

> Let us not be afraid of failure,
> but let us be afraid of being successful
> in things that don't matter. [1]

When thoughts of FAILURE assault the mind, we can be left staggering from the blow. Thoughts of failing in life, failing your family, failing the Lord can be crippling and devastating. "Failure" is a word we avoid when evaluating ourselves; no one wants to be a failure. As frightening as it may seem, though, failure is the brutal rock on which God often sharpens his people for true success—success as *God* defines success.

Failure and the fear of failing create powerful emotions in the heart; the reality, or perceived reality, can be crushing. Consequently, society is on a success craze, but sadly, *success*, as the world defines it, at any cost. There are countless people who'll teach you how to think positively and be successful, for a price of course. There are books, CDs, DVDs, you name it, on how to succeed at anything. All promise success and not failure; in most cases, the person selling the books and tapes is the only success, not the purchaser. I read where one fellow offered to sell his books on "How to Succeed" for a month's room and board; I guess success can be defined by a lot of different standards.

People, especially in America, have tremendous difficulty acknowledging and coping with failure, even though it is very often a necessary part of real success. We're quick to see it in others, but not in ourselves. Thomas Edison had hundreds of failed experiments when trying to invent the battery. He looked upon those seeming failures as hundreds of successes. He told one of his employees that he had successfully found hundreds of ways it wouldn't work.

It's hard for adults to be realistic about failure. Have you ever watched a child learning to walk? Watch that child and you'll see failure after failure. Watch a youngster learn to hit a baseball or play golf: what do you see? You see failure after failure. How well did you do when you learned to ride a bike? Did you simply get on it the first time and peddle down the road? How many times did you fail before you learned the art of keeping your balance? Life is a series of failures, but all failure is not bad, and not all success is good. I once heard the late Vance Havner say: "Success can feather our nest so comfortably that we forget how to fly." Failure is one of the instruments used by our Lord to humble us, to mature us, to prepare us for greater mountains to climb, and to kill the pride of self-sufficiency. One of the greatest errors of our day is over-confidence. Confidence can be good and needful, but, King Over-Confidence is easily toppled by failures. Our confidence must be in Christ. How impatient are the creatures; the Creator is in no hurry. It takes a long time to grow a fruit-bearing tree and it sometimes requires a lot of pruning.

Webster defines Success as "a favorable or satisfactory outcome or result." Does that mean that if a person makes a lot of money and owns a lot of houses and stuff that he is a success? Most societies in the world define success by power, money, and fame. If a person is famous for sports ability, acting talent, or some other great accomplishment, the general public says "that's success!" Is it really? Does power, money, fame, or accomplishments guarantee a happy ending in life?

What is the measure of success or failure? No Christian can define success or failure without knowing how God defines success and failure. What is our compass to point the way? Our purpose for even being here is given in Scripture: we are to obey God, we are to glorify God in all that we do, and we are to enjoy God forever.

> *Let us hear the conclusion of the whole matter: Fear God and keep His commandments, for this is the whole duty of man.* (Ecclesiastes 12:12, NKJV)

> *Whether, then you eat or drink or whatever you do, do all to the glory of God.*
> (1 Corinthians 10:31)

> *Whom have I in heaven but you? And besides You, I desire nothing on earth. My flesh and my heart may fail, but God is the strength of my heart and my portion forever.* (Psalm 73:25-26)

Obeying God, glorifying God, and enjoying God are the Creator's purpose for man. According to His Word this *must* be our ambition. If not, there's no real success no matter how much glitter and sparkle the world sees in any accomplishment. There can never be true happiness apart from the intentions of the Creator: obedience to God, glorifying God, and seeking to enjoy Him forever. To paraphrase a statement by C.S. Lewis, "The ultimate failure in life is to be successful in things that don't matter." To walk in the path that leads to true success, as defined by Scripture, we have to know what the Bible teaches.

> No man is uneducated who knows the Bible,
> and no one is wise who is ignorant of its teachings. [2]

A graphic picture of failure and deliverance is found in the story of Israel in the Old Testament book of Exodus. The people of God had been slaves in Egypt then delivered by God. They experienced three distinct events from which we can learn, not unlike three stages in our sanctification as Christians. They went from salvation from Egypt to struggles and failings in the wilderness.

> The Red Sea experience: separation from Egypt
> The wilderness experience: humbling and teaching
> The crossing over Jordan: living and conquering by faith

When we were redeemed, we came through the Red Sea which separated us from Egypt (the world), but then comes the wilderness. The Israelites wandered in the desert for 40 years. Why? Was it purposeless? The answer is recorded in the book of Deuteronomy as follows:

> *You shall remember all the way which the Lord your God has led you in the wilderness these forty years,* **that He might humble you,** *testing you,* **to know what was in your heart, whether** *you would keep His commandments or not.* **He humbled you and let you be hungry,** *and fed you with manna which you did not know, nor did your fathers know, that He might make you understand that man does not live by bread alone, but man lives by everything that proceeds out of the mouth of the Lord.* (Deuteronomy 8:2-3, emphasis mine)

Picture the situation. God had delivered these people from bondage (Deuteronomy 8:14). They were slaves, but now free. But they complain and grumble and disobey. It's in the wilderness that we learn a lot about ourselves and about the greatness of God. Israel was in the wilderness for forty years when it was, at most, only an eleven day journey to the Promised Land. This was God's study course on *Man's Failure and God's Sufficiency*. God never does anything without a purpose and nothing is ever done without God; therefore, everything has a purpose.

In the wilderness, we learn what's in our heart. *"That He might humble you, testing you, to know what was in your heart, whether you would keep His commandments or not"* (Deuteronomy 8:2). Weaknesses must be seen and experienced; man won't trust God until he has to. As long as there's one ounce of hope in self, man will not trust the Lord. We must be humbled and our hearts exposed; God often does that in the wilderness of DarkLand. The struggles and failings in the wilderness don't come so that HE can find out what's in our hearts, but that WE might find out what's there (see John 2:25). Trials and failures stir and strike the heart so the snakes will come out of their hiding places. It may be frightening, but it's necessary. In this exposure we begin to see what Paul meant when he said, *"I know that nothing good dwells in me, that is, in my flesh; for the willing is present in me, but the doing of good is not"* (Romans 7:18). He also knew where His strength lay, *"I can do all things through Him who strengthens me"* (Philippians 4:13).

One of the most profitable experiences in the lives of God's children is learning what they are by nature and the necessity for the grace of God in their lives to guide, instruct, and sustain them. When brought to that state, we become fit vessels to be used by the Lord. Until then, men are self-serving or, at best, immature—a failing grade in God's University of Life.

In the wilderness, we are taught. The Lord told the Israelites, I *"let you be hungry..."* Why did He do that? *"That He might make you understand that man does not live by bread alone, but man lives by everything that proceeds out of the mouth of the Lord"* (Deuteronomy 8:3). He sometimes lets our souls hunger until we are ready to eat the heavenly manna—Christ. *"Jesus said to them, 'I am the bread of life; he who comes to Me will not hunger, and he who believes in Me will never thirst'"* (John 6:35). He may allow your soul to wander around in the wilderness of the philosophies of this world until you learn that there's no bread there. There are only two kinds of life, physical and spiritual, and the source of both is the Lord Jesus Christ. Man's thinking must be put in order. He must learn to think scripturally about himself and about the Lord and about the circumstances the Lord places him in; he must be taught by God.

In the wilderness, the soul will be encouraged. *"In the wilderness He fed you manna which your fathers did not know, that He might humble you and that He might test you, to do good for you in the end"* (Deuteronomy 8:16). We ought not grumble and complain, but those evils are often first and swiftest to surface in times of darkness. Scripture tells us that we should give thanks for the circumstance the Lord places us in. He does not take us into waters that are over our heads to drown us, but to cleanse us and ultimately encourage us. Afflictions associated with failures are necessary to prepare us to face the difficulties of life and to drive us to the Word of God. David said, *"Before I was afflicted I went astray, But now I keep Your word"* (Psalm 119:67). This is a tough school and we all start out as dunces, but God will not let you flunk. If He has brought you out of Egypt (the world), He will take you into His eternal country, His Celestial City. The road on which we travel to get there may be cluttered with wilderness experiences, dark and threatening stretches of rocky terrain, but we don't pitch our tents there. He will lead us—revealing our hearts, educating our minds, and encouraging our souls. True success comes only from Him.

Another illustration is clearly seen in the New Testament. An experience in the life of Peter exposed his heart, taught him, and encouraged him. (See Luke 5:1-11.) Peter was somewhat cocky and impetuous. Peter and his friends had fished all night but caught nothing. They were professional fishermen, had the best equipment, experience, and knowledge to catch fish; on this night they failed miserably.

The next morning, no doubt very tired, frustrated, and feeling the pangs of failure, Peter and the others were washing their nets when Jesus came to him and said, "Peter, I'd like to use your boat for a while." The Lord stepped into Peter's boat and asked him to push out a bit from the shore of the lake. From this platform Jesus preached to the people on shore. Then turning to Peter and his friends Jesus said, "Let's go fishing, boys!" *"Put out into the deep water and let down your nets for a catch."* With mixed emotions Peter replied, *"Master, we worked hard all night and caught nothing, but I will do as you say and let down the nets."* In other words, "Lord, we know how to fish, and there are no fish here, but I'll do what you say." It's obvious that Peter was reluctant. But when he obeyed, the results were overwhelming; *"they enclosed a great quantity of fish, and their nets began to break; so they signaled to their partners in the other boat for them to come and help them And they came and filled both of the boats, so that they began to sink"* (Luke 5:6-7). Peter was humbled, amazed, and afraid.

Now let's compare the two fishing expeditions recorded in Luke 5. We have the same lake, the same boats, the same, nets and the same fishermen. In the night, when fishing is best, they were failures; the next day, in obedience to Christ, they were successful. There's no question that Peter's heart was exposed, he learned things he needed to know, and he was encouraged. Failure in the night was the backdrop for the precious lesson of success and dependence on Him who is Lord over all things, even the sea and fish. Peter learned the lesson. Falling at the feet of Jesus, he said, *"'Go away from me Lord, for I am a sinful man.' For amazement had seized him and all his companions..."* (Luke 5:8, 9). To see Christ for *Who He is* always brings this reaction—amazement and deep awareness of sin in the Face of Holiness.

God wants you to be a success in what He's called you to do, and the path may take you right through failure. What turned Peter and his friends from failure to achievement? Jesus was in the boat with them. The presence of the Lord made the difference; they weren't working in their own wisdom. If you want to be successful, you must have Jesus in the "boat" with you. I'm not talking about a "Sunday morning religion." Peter's boat was his livelihood, his business, his occupation, and he made it available for the Lord's use. The Lord used Peter's business as a platform from which to preach. Does the Lord have access to your job? Is your livelihood, business, or occupation available at all times for Him to use? Is He able to minister through you in everything you do and wherever you are? You cannot privatize God's activities in your life. Christ will be Lord *of all* or He won't be Lord *at all*. Faith in the Lord Jesus is total commitment: all or nothing. "Christ never comes next." (Vance Havner) All we are and have are His; we are stewards of those gifts.

Obedience precedes blessing and revelation. Peter makes His boat available for the Lord's use; Jesus uses that same boat to supply a great catch to supply Peter's needs.

On the second fishing expedition, Peter and his friends followed the directions of the Master Fisherman. He told them *where, when,* and *how* to fish. Even though the Lord's command didn't make sense to them—as seasoned fishermen, they knew the heat of the day was the worst time to fish—nevertheless they obeyed. We won't always understand God's plans and purposes, but we aren't told to understand everything; we're commanded to obey His Word: *"but I will do as You say ... "* (Luke 5:5).

Peter certainly did not expect so great a blessing as he received, but he may have expected something. There are always anticipated blessings when we listen to Him and do what His Word says. With every command, there is a blessing promised if obeyed. *"Put out into the deep water and let down your nets for a catch"* (Luke 5:4).

When we have the Lord present in our boat, His plan in our head, His promises in our heart, success will follow—God's kind of success. Don't complain when the Lord puts you through a dark wilderness of failure; He's doing something in your life. He may be *exposing* some things. He certainly is *teaching* you some things. And He will *encourage* you in His own time.

Never underestimate the effect of failure. Failure and the fears that accompany it can be powerful emotions, but are part of life. For the Christian, what is labeled "failure" may, in fact, be the learning experience necessary for true success.

> We tend to run away from the things that make us. We should neither court suffering nor complain about it. Instead, we should see it as one of the means God chooses to employ in order to make us increasingly useful to the Master. It is from this perspective that James urges his readers to "consider it pure joy whenever you face trials of many kinds" (James 1:2).
>
> Often, we can adopt such an attitude only in looking back. Many times the immediate sense of failure and disappointment is so overwhelming that we are unable to grasp the benefit package. We need to remember this when talking to our friends who are in the eye of the storm. [3]

Too often we allow failure to escort us into the dark shadows of despair, discouragement, and sometimes even into depression. Failures are to be learned from, but not used as a pattern. Failure may thrust us into DarkLand, but we're not to build our house there.

How do we do that? How do we find our way out when we're slapped into the wilderness by failure? First, beware of two assailants that stay in the shadows until they detect failure—they jump out and make circumstances even more difficult. They are *people* and *self*. When you think you've failed there is always someone ready to make you feel like a permanent loser, criticizing and playing the blame-game. It may be someone else, or it may be you! We are not perfect. We are not spiritual super-stars. But we are sinners saved by grace and loved by God Himself. We are all "failures" enrolled by the King into the University of Christ and are learning to be successful.

> *Come to Me, all who are weary and heavy laden, and I will give you rest. Take My yoke upon you and learn from Me, for I am gentle and humble in heart, and you will find rest for your souls. For My yoke is easy and My burden is light.* (Matthew 11:28-30).

Christ is building His kingdom with earth's broken things. Men want only the strong, the successful, the victorious, and the unbroken—in building their kingdoms. But God is the God of the broken, the unsuccessful, of those who have failed. Heaven is filling with earth's broken lives, and there is no 'bruised reed' which Christ cannot take and restore to glorious blessedness and beauty. He can take the life crushed by pain or sorrow—and make it into a harp whose music shall be all praise. He can lift earth's saddest failure up to heaven's glory! [4]

What do you expect from yourself? Are you realistic in your expectations? Pressure from outside and pressure from within are often the offspring of a preoccupation with "out of reach" standards or preoccupation with Self. Expectations beyond your God given abilities lead to frustration at best, and failure most likely. Are your expectations scriptural? Are you submitted to God's will for you?

Psalm 103 gives practical principles and light for right thinking. David was Israel's greatest king and a man after God's own heart, but David faced some harsh circumstances and personally failed many times during his lifetime. He learned how to respond rightly to both perceived failure and personal failure. Psalm 103 is thought to have been composed by David while he was fleeing for his life and being hunted by King Saul. Truly the circumstances appeared dire, but consider carefully how he reacted. First he had a talk with himself, and then he meditated on the Lord and His mercies. When he was down, David went to the Lord.

Your right reaction to failure is your responsibility; it's not the duty of your wife, husband, pastor, or anyone else. Others may contribute to your failure, but you alone are responsible in your attitude and reaction. Turn your heart toward Him. Replace self-pity, guilt, and unreasonable standards with thinking about the love, grace, and mercy of the Lord. Assurance comes by looking to Christ. Scottish preacher Robert Murray M'Cheyne said, "Learn much of the Lord Jesus. For every look at yourself, take ten looks at Christ."

Men place conditions on their accolades and rewards, but God's grace is unconditional. Psalm 103 describes the character of One who loves us and cares for us—no unrealistic demands. Go to Him again and again; the Fountain of Living Water never runs dry or bitter. Christ is the friend of sinners and outcasts.

Failure creates insecurity. It causes us to feel insignificant, unproductive, and incapable. But the Lord knows us inside and out. He pities us without criticizing us. We are His children. He knows that, at our best, we are but dust. He does not expect too much or too little from us. By His grace, He equips you for all that He commands. Security and assurance do not lie within ourselves, but in Him. Regardless of what appears to be failure, the path of obedience is the path of safety.

Refuse to compare yourself with other people. We fight this battle every time we fail. We look at others who seem to be such great successes with little effort. But our insight is so limited and prone to sinful jealousies. Our duty is to follow Christ and to think scripturally.

Perspective is simply how you look at life and evaluate it. What one person considers success may be a failure to another. If your perspective comes from the opinions of men, you will most likely consider yourself a failure. But if you take God's perspective on life you will come out with an accurate evaluation. In His plans and purpose you are going through life's experiences in preparation for glory; you're being molded and polished.

David looks within, then he looks up—meditating and focusing on the grace, love, and mercy of God. He ends Psalm 103 in awe and worship declaring the sovereignty of God over everything. Nothing encourages more than knowing that God is on His throne of power and is working all things out for my good and His glory (Romans 8:28).

Christ is not a failure and we are connected to Him. What may seem to be utter failure to us may be necessary to achieve His ends. It's better to fail in something that will ultimately succeed, than to succeed in something that will ultimately fail. Our goal is spiritual; it is heavenly, not earthly. Our total success will come when we're made like the Lord Jesus Christ in thought, word, and action. We have been predestinated to that end; it *will* come to pass.

> *For those whom He foreknew, He also predestinated to become conformed to the image of His Son, so that He would be the firstborn among many brethren.* (Romans 8:29)

> We are often tossed and driven
> On the restless sea of time.
> Somber skies and howling tempests
> oft succeed a bright sunshine.
> In that land of perfect day,
> When the mists have rolled away,
> We will understand it better by and by.
>
> We are often destitute
> Of the things that life demands;
> Want of food and want of shelter,
> thirsty hills and barren lands.
> We are trusting in the Lord
> And according to God's Word
> We will understand it better by and by.
>
> Trials dark on every hand,
> And we cannot understand
> All the ways that God would lead us
> to that blessed promised land;
> But He'll guide us with His eye,
> And we'll follow till we die;
> We will understand it better by and by.
>
> Oft our cherished plans have failed,
> Disappointments have prevailed,

And we've wandered in the darkness,
heavyhearted and alone;
But we're trusting in the Lord,
And, according to His word,
We will understand it better by and by.

Temptations, hidden snares,
Often take us unawares,
And our hearts are made to bleed
for some thoughtless word or deed,
And we wonder why the test
When we try to do our best,
But we will understand it better by and by.

By and by, when the morning comes,
When the saints of God are gathered home,
We will tell the story how we've overcome;
We will understand it better by and by. (5)

---

1 Author Unknown
2 Samuel Chadwick, *The Speakers Quote Book*, Roy B. Zuck, Kregel Publications, p. 46
3 Alistair Begg, *Made For His Pleasure*, Moody Press, 1966, p. 109
4 J.R. Miller, gracegems.org/miller
5 Charles Tindley (1851–1933), *We'll Understand It Better By and By*, United Methodist Hymnal, #525

6

DISCOURAGEMENT

If the excuse for fainting be that the work is toilsome, that it is too much a drag upon you, why did you begin it? You ought to have known this at the first. You should have counted the cost. But let me add, the work was not toilsome when your heart was loving, neither would it now be so hard if your soul were right with God. [1]

Once upon a time it was announced that the devil was going out of business and would sell all the tools of his trade to anyone willing to pay the price. All his tools were cleverly and attractively displayed on the day of the big sale. *Envy, hatred, jealousy, malice, deceit, sensuality, and pride* were among the many implements of evil laid out by Satan, each tool marked with its own price. In the corner was a harmless looking wedge-shaped and well-worn tool, yet it bore a higher price than any of the others. The devil was asked what it was. He answered, "Discouragement." The next question came quickly, "But why is it so highly priced even though it's plain to see that it is old and worn out?" Laughing, the devil replied, "Discouragement is more useful and effective to me than any of my other tools. I can pry open and get into a heart and mind with discouragement when I cannot get near with any other tool. Once I get inside a human with discouragement, I can sway and torture in whatever way suits me best. It is well worn because I use it on everyone and few people ever know that it belongs to me."

This tool was so highly priced that no one was able to buy it; to this day it has never been sold. It still belongs to the devil, and he still uses it on Adam's children with great success. Although the author of this illustration is unknown, the story surely contains much truth.

Why does discouragement hold such a high place in Satan's arsenal? Let us unmask this parasite that can attach itself to our mind, drain our energy and steal our peace if left unchecked. There are at least three attributes of discouragement that undergird its power.

First, Discouragement is universal. Adam was created and placed in the perfect environment of the Garden of Eden, a place of comfort and happiness. Then God created Eve from the side of Adam and brought her to Adam to be his wife. They were to live and enjoy this perfect environment and populate the earth. But Eve listened to the serpent and influenced her husband Adam to eat from the Tree of the Knowledge of Good and Evil—and sin entered. In that act of disobedience to God's law, Adam and all his descendants became sinful by nature and by act. As the representative of the human race, Adam's sinful nature was passed to all who would proceed from him through all the generations of man. Consequently, we are fallen creatures. Sin not only invaded the human race, but it has taken the human race prisoner, establishing every descendant of Adam to be a sinner by nature. *"Therefore, just as through one man sin entered into the world and death through sin and so death spread to all men, because all sinned..." (*Romans 5:12). Listen to Francis Schaeffer's words concerning this:

> By the action of one man in a historic, space-time situation, sin entered into the world of men. But this is not just a theoretical statement that gives us a reasonable and sufficient answer to man's present dilemma, explaining how the world can be so evil and

God still be good. It is that in reality, from this time on, man was and is a sinner. Though some men do not like the teaching, the Bible continues like a sledgehammer driving home the fact that evil has entered into the world of man, all men are now sinners, all men now sin." [2]

As the result of our sinfulness, discouragement has power. As surely as sin is common in the human race, so is discouragement. Each of us is prone to depend on our own strength, intellect and abilities. This inevitably leads to discouragement. Life in a fallen cursed world is laced with peril and failure making us ripe for discouragement. No one is exempt; we all will travel on discouragement's ground.

Second, Discouragement is recurring. Discouragement will come again and again and again. In this life you will never outgrow the tendency to become discouraged. Scripture clearly reminds us that we are fallen helpless creatures apart from Christ. When people say, "I get discouraged so easily," what they're really saying is that discouragement is recurring in their lives. Unfortunately most people seem to come out of one set of circumstances which disheartens them, then without any pause go into another set of circumstances which brings or pushes them farther down into Discouragement's territory. We will experience endless episodes of discouragement if we do not learn how to deal scripturally with adverse circumstances and failures.

Third, Discouragement is highly contagious. You can, and too often do, give the problem to others around you. Have you ever been to a "Discouragement Party" where people sit around and tell each other all the reasons they are discouraged? The conversation is negative and hopeless. Who wouldn't become discouraged in such an atmosphere? Discouragement is contagious and the Bible warns us about spreading it. *"Who is the man that is afraid and fainthearted (discouraged)? Let him depart and return to his house, so that he might not make his brothers' hearts melt like his heart"* (Deuteronomy 20:8). If you spend a lot of time with discouraged and negative people, most likely you also will become habitually discouraged. You can become a carrier of the malady passing it on to those around you. Without God's light in the Scripture to lead, you join the Club of the Discouraged gathering around and swapping tales of despair. Far too often family, friends, and even church family can become disheartened when exposed repeatedly to sinful discouragement. William Cowper wrote the following in his poem *To Mary*:

> But ah! By constant heed I know
> How oft the sadness that I show
> Transforms thy smiles to looks of woe,
> My Mary!
>
> And should my future lot be cast
> With much resemblance of the past,
> Thy worn-out heart will break at last,
> My Mary! [3]

Both Christians and unbelievers are found here in the DarkLand of discouraged people. The unbeliever may be more prone to become discouraged since he sees no hope for his circumstances; God's child will become discouraged too. Nevertheless, in our time of "illness" we have the Right Physician and the Right Medicines. Christ is our Physician and His word and providence are our medicines. He is the Christian's solid and unchanging ground of hope. People outside the realm of the redeemed in Christ have nothing on which they can rely for realistic hope. The world's wisdom is a charlatan whose advice leads only to hopelessness and false light.

But why do Christians who have hope in Christ get discouraged? The answer is this: they have taken their eyes off Christ. Do you remember the story of Peter walking on the water? (Matthew 14:28-33) He was doing great until he took his eyes off Christ and began to look at the storm and waves surrounding him, then he began to sink. Like Peter, a believer may look away from Christ and glance around at circumstances and unfamiliar surroundings, the stormy sea of life and rising waves of darkness. With his eyes off the source of strength and encouragement, he begins to sink into danger and discouragement. We have no ability to walk on the stormy seas of life without a loving Savior to sustain us. Without our eyes constantly and persistently fixed on Him, we sink farther down into darkness. Most all trails into DarkLand merge into discouragement.

So, discouragement is *universal*—no one is exempt. Discouragement is *recurring*—visiting us several times in our lives on this earth. And discouragement is *contagious*—you can catch it from other discouraged people and you can pass it on.

The word "discouragement" is a compound word having two parts. The first part is *"dis"* which means "to lose" or "the loss of"; the second part is obviously *"courage."* Put these two parts together and you have "the loss of courage" thus "discouragement"; the loss of courage to face present adverse circumstances. The Bible uses the word "fainthearted" to describe this condition. To be fainthearted or discouraged is to be in a state of defeat and, I might add, living next door to Mr. Depression. It is but a small step from stress to discouragement to depression. During the first Gulf War, which freed Kuwait from the occupying soldiers of Iraq, the Iraqi soldiers gave up fighting and surrendered en masse because they lost courage. They were fainthearted and overwhelmed by the oncoming coalition armed forces; in their despair, the Iraqis gave up. They lost courage.

In Nehemiah chapter four we find some of the *Causes* and the *Cures* for the problem of discouragement. Nehemiah was the able leader of the Jewish group who had been given permission to leave captivity and return to Jerusalem to rebuild the wall around the devastated city. This highly privileged group of people came to the task with great zeal and excitement. In their minds, they were going to restore the ruined city of Jerusalem to its former glory days. But they soon became discouraged even though their goal was good and right. What were the causes of their discouragement and what were the cures? To answer, let the Lord speak to us through His word.

Causes for Discouragement
There were at least four causes which brought these people in Nehemiah 4 into discouragement. These causes are generally the same pits of quicksand that pull you and me down into discouragement. Let's examine each one.

Fatigue
The first cause for discouragement is very often *fatigue*: being just plain physically tired. In Nehemiah 4:6 we read that the workers were *"strong hearted"* or *"had a mind to work"*—the opposite of fatigue. When they began they were excited in their anticipation of the wall being built and the city restored; their hearts and minds were in their work. They could envision the return of the glory days for Israel. They worked long and hard, full of courage. But then they became fatigued. Then Scripture says, *"the strength of the burden bearers is failing..."* (Nehemiah 4:10): they were tired, worn out physically and emotionally drained. The workers were worn out and consequently were losing courage. Without adequate rest, fatigue sets in and courage wanes.

There are no less than 250 places where the word "rest" is used in the New Testament. From analyzing those references, one thing is very clear—rest is absolutely necessary; the Lord wants us to have adequate rest for our bodies and minds.

Sometimes the most spiritual and sensible thing you can do is go to bed, relax, and get a good night's sleep. Take a day off, go bike riding, fishing, hiking, or golfing. But our culture seems to work in the opposite way. People are constantly on the move and many homes have become no more than boarding houses. Home has become only a place for our children, as well as the parents, to eat and sleep. In America the average father spends much less than one hour a day dedicated to his children—their only contact is seeing each other when one is coming in and the other is going out. If this is true in family life, how much more true is it in our modern day church life? Our society has become a fast moving and impatient society. If we don't find some way to slow down and take a rest we will crash. We cannot continue in such an exhausting pace.

When do most people become fatigued and discouraged? Note Nehemiah 4:6. They had built the wall halfway up: *"the wall was joined together to half its height..."* "Half-done" is a common place for fatigue and discouragement to find a foothold. By the time half the task is completed the novelty has worn off—boredom has set in—life settles down into a rut—a routine—a ritual. Fatigue and discouragement are on the horizon and ready to rush in like the ocean's waters surging over the broken seawalls of New Orleans during hurricane Katrina.

When my daughter Susan was seven, I remember how excited she would get when we started planning for a trip. When we actually began she would be very enthusiastic looking at all the scenery as we drove along. But when we got a good distance into the trip she would begin getting bored, tired, and discouraged. That's when the questions started, "Daddy, are we there yet? How much further is it?" Christian life is a life-long battle against becoming weary in well doing and fending off discouragement. Slow down, rest, focus your mind and heart on the Lord, and never look away.

Frustration

A second cause of discouragement is *frustration*; it can ride upon fatigue. In Nehemiah 4:10, the people said *"there is much rubbish; and we ourselves are unable to rebuild the wall."* They were both fatigued and frustrated; the union of the two was DISCOURAGEMENT.

The men were building a new wall but rubbish and broken pieces of the old wall lay in heaps everywhere. Because they looked at the mass of rubbish still surrounding them their spirits became crushed and enthusiasm drained away. They were only half-way finished but already tired. They no longer had the vision of the finished work, but rather the enormous weight of work still to be done; they became frustrated.

We may have rubbish all around us. "Rubbish" is defined in a host of ways: wreckage, remains, fragments, garbage, debris, junk. Past failures may plague the mind, especially if preceded by fatigue. And, oh, how past failures linger in our memory—the wreckage of goals crushed or desires never realized. The remains of bad decisions and their consequences may produce mountains of regret. Life becomes one big frustration and discouragement.

An inadequate view of the Scriptures, of God, of Christ, of the Holy Spirit, and of ourselves is rubbish that will pile up and distort our thinking and lead quickly to frustration. The Word of God clearly defines us as fallen, depraved, helpless sinners. Apart from that understanding there can be no adequate view of God, His grace, love and mercy, all of which are wrapped up in the Person of Christ. This rubbish is perhaps the most deadly.

> Scriptures are profuse in describing for us God's person, His character, and how He has chosen to reveal Himself. In mining the wealth of that content we come to understand how profoundly He has responded to the cry of the human heart—'Who are You God?' This ought to be the paramount quest of every man, woman and child, because from that knowledge flows every other answer to the cries of the heart and mind. 'Who are You God?' begets contrary answers when left at the mercy of individual whims. [4]

Confused priorities, doing good things at the expense of essential things, will surely bring fatigue and frustration. Too many earthly and temporal activities can leave us so tired we neglect time with the Lord, Bible study, and prayer. Few things are more frustrating than knowing the right path but never seeming to be able to get on it. I am convinced that one of the main causes of fatigue and discouragement in the lives of many Christians today is their total absorption with events and activities of their children. They do all the "good things" with their children at the expense of doing the essential things: church attendance, consistent Bible study, seeking the Lord in prayer, spending time together at home as a family, and talking about the truths of Scripture and how to live by them.

There is no getting out of the dark or clearing away the rubbish without the Word of God which is our map and compass. We see the wreckage of ruined lives, shattered by alcohol, drugs, divorce, child abuse, murder. Our existence in this world is a walk through the rubbish of corruption in every area. Is it any wonder that we are prone to become discouraged? We are not unlike the people in Nehemiah's day. In their tiredness they focused on the heaps of rubbish around them and the work yet to be done. They became frustrated and discouraged.

Failures
A third contributor to discouragement is *failure*. Although temporary, the builders were failures at the point when they said, *"we cannot rebuild the wall."* Their plans were not going as well as anticipated. Fatigue and frustration clouded their minds and they saw themselves as failures. "We can't do it, so we are going to give up and quit!" They had lost their faith in the God who had allowed them to leave Babylon to rebuild the wall and they became afraid of their enemies.

Everyone fails; the big question is, how do we handle failure? How prone we are to sit down and have ourselves a pity party where we are the featured speaker! "O poor ME, everything always goes wrong for ME, no one understands ME and how I feel, I just can't go on...!" And our speech usually digresses to blaming others.

Let me illustrate with an all too common situation. Mr. and Mrs. Young Christian love each other and love the Lord, study His Word, and worship with their church family. They work, plan, and begin a family. Everyday living changes quickly as new and beautiful "additions" come to the couple. Expenses increase; days become filled with careers, diapers, doctor visits, pre-school, first grade, homework, PTA, ballet lessons, little league practice, little league games, little league make-up games, middle school, committee meetings. There is no time for Sunday night with their church; they squeeze in vacation days. There is no time for family time and Bible reading; they are too tired to get up every Sunday for church. Days become filled with flu, dentist appointments, sporadic bickering, teen backtalk and rebellion, fatigue, frustration—failure—discouragement. What happened? When?

Doing good things at the expense of essential things brings on fatigue, frustration, failure, and discouragement. Once taken, even a slight detour from the straight and narrow path of Scripture will lead down and down into DarkLand. So is failure a final destination? For the Christian it must never be. Failure may be a place we visit, but never a place to pitch our tents and live.

Sometimes the cause of failure is hard to pinpoint, and may not be the result of disobedience. Remember Thomas Edison's story in the chapter called *Failure*? After trying hundreds of different ways to create a dry cell battery, it is said that one of Thomas Edison's workers tried to persuade him to give up. Edison replied that they had not failed; rather, they had been successful in discovering hundreds of ways it wouldn't work. Thomas Edison eventually made the battery. Failure to Edison was not something to get discouraged about, it was a necessary means to success. God causes or allows every trial that comes to us. He uses them as tools. Each trial is to mold us into the image of His Son. As we pass each test, He moves us along to a higher plain in our spiritual maturity. Failure is one of those trials. Learn how to use the failures in life to draw closer to Christ and His Word.

Fear
The fourth donor to discouragement is *fear*. In Nehemiah 4:11-12, Fear joins fatigue, frustration, and failure in assaulting the people of God. In verse eleven the cause of their fear is stated: enemies living nearby. The wall represented protection for God's people, so the enemy criticized and ridiculed the builders (vs. 1-3), then threatened (v. 11), saying *"we will kill you if you continue building that wall."* The workers became frightened and discouraged (v. 14).

The first to become frightened and discouraged were people living nearest to the enemy (v. 12); those who would suffer first if the enemy carried out their threats. Fatigued, frustrated, failing, and now frightened, they soon discouraged the others, for fear is contagious.

Are your fears discouraging you? Economic fears? Your income is uncertain. You only have enough money coming in to pay your bills each month. There's never any left for vacations or doing some of the things you have always dreamed of doing. Finances dwindle. Bills pile up. Physical fears? Sickness or physical disease keeps you down and frightened. Emotional or spiritual fears? The struggle is ultimately the spiritual battleground in your life. Are you emotionally drained because of painful circumstances in your family, a death of a loved one, a wayward child, etc.? The list can be endless of the things that can cause us to fear or become discouraged. How do we handle these circumstances? At least three reactions are possible, each with very different outcomes.

> You can move against it in anger and become bitter.
> You can move away from it with more fear and become discouraged.
> You can move into it with faith in Christ, and have victory.

Four causes of discouragement are: *fatigue, frustration, failure,* and *fear.* These are common foes in every person's life, and lure us farther and deeper into discouragement apart from God's grace and a focus on the Savior and His Word.

Cures for Discouragement

God gave insight to Nehemiah to evaluate and understand the situation. The task was great and the task was right, but the workers were fatigued, frustrated, failing, and fearful. Wisdom for discouragements and difficult tasks will always be provided although God's timing, and His providences move in mysterious ways. Three principles were used by Nehemiah and are equally as applicable to us today: *reorganize, remember,* and *resist.*

Reorganize
The first principle Nehemiah exercised was to reorganize the workers.

> *Then I stationed men in the lowest parts of the space behind the wall, the exposed places, and I stationed the people in families with their swords, spears and bows. When I saw their fear, I rose and spoke to the nobles, the officials and the rest of the people: "Do not be afraid of them; remember the Lord who is great and awesome and fight for your brothers, your sons, your daughters, your wives and your houses."*
> (Nehemiah 4:13-14)

He saw their fatigue, their mounting frustrations, their perceptions of failure, and especially their paralyzing fear of enemy opposition. He recognized that something had to change if the people were to be strengthened and effectively resume the work of building the wall.

When a football team goes into the locker room at half time and is trailing in the score, it's time to reorganize. In the first half they may have executed their game plans very well; if they are lagging behind in the score and the players are discouraged, something isn't working. A good coach must formulate a new line of attack for the second half—he reorganizes the team with a new second half strategy.

What happened to these people in the book of Nehemiah is similar to the football team. They had enthusiastically labored to produce the first half of the wall, but the enthusiasm and energy were spent. Now they were tired, frustrated, felt like they had failed, and the threats and mocking of their enemies melted their hearts in fear. Reorganization did not become necessary because the people were doing the wrong thing. On the contrary, they were doing the right thing; they were obeying God. But still they were discouraged. Even if they were forced to continue as they were, progress would be slow and tedious and the wall would not be well-built and strong. Likewise, when we become tired, fearful, and discouraged, we will likely get an inferior result regardless of what work we're doing even in the spiritual realm.

When discouraged it's time to step back and take a good look at what we're doing and in what attitude we're doing it. Ask questions, "Am I doing the right thing? Am I doing it God's way? Is my attitude right?" If the answer to any of these questions is "no," then pray and reorganize.

Nehemiah carefully analyzed and reorganized. He put the workmen with their main support group—their families. When will you fight hardest against an enemy? The answer is simple—when it's personal—when you're fighting for your families: *"fight for your brothers, your sons, your daughters, your wives and your house."* Remember your family and the consequences of giving up the fight. Love and devotion in defense of those we love will almost certainly reenergize and encourage. A soldier fights hardest when fighting for his country and family. Love will rise to persevere against all apparent odds. As Christians, Christ Jesus is our great General and cannot fail; we are His soldiers and are enlisted for the duration of the war. We are to *"fight the good fight of faith"* (1 Timothy 6:12). Paul said, *"I have fought the good fight, I have finished the course, I have kept the faith"* (Timothy 4:7). Despite numerous discouraging events in his life, the Apostle never gave in, never gave out, and never gave up. The Christian life in a sinful world is a battle. Never forget that and never lay your weapons down. Always be on the alert. Conquered ground has to be held.

Remember
The second principle in fighting discouragement is to remember some things. Remember who you are in the sight of God. Remember

who He is, what He has done, and what He has promised in His Word. *"Do not be afraid...remember the Lord who is great and awesome..."* (v. 14). You are a member of the Royal Family of Heaven, a redeemed, blood-bought child of God. The King of kings has promised to provide your every need for now and for eternity. Remembering that the Lord is sovereign in all His love, power, and authority will instill courage in the heart and mind regardless of the circumstances surrounding us.

>Remember His goodness to you in the past.
>Remember His closeness to you in the present.
>Remember His promises for you in the future.

Remember also that your thoughts about a circumstance trigger emotions and emotions lead to action or reaction. Thinking scripturally is critical in every circumstance whether we are in conflict or on what seems to be peaceful ground. When we find ourselves in depths of discouragement we are probably not thinking scripturally. Note the following sequence regarding a circumstance in your life:

>*Circumstance > Thoughts > Emotions > Reaction*

Circumstances do not cause discouragement, but rather how you think about and react to the circumstances.

Listen to what encouraged Paul, *"I can do all things through Christ who strengthens me"* (Philippians 4:13). Nothing *"will be able to separate me from the love of God which is in Christ Jesus"* (Romans 8:39). *"...If God is for us, who can be against us..."* (Romans 8:13). These are only a few of the promises we can grasp and hang on to in times of difficulty and despair. Remember His promises.

Remember what the Lord Jesus Christ has done for us in the past, what He is doing for us now, and what He promises for the future.

He died for us, shedding His *rich, red, royal,* and *redeeming* blood to atone for our sins. He is at this moment seated at the right hand of God on the throne of Heaven ruling over His universe, interceding for us and providing our every need. He has promised that He will come again and take us home to be with Him for eternity. He indwells us through the Holy Spirit to help us call to mind all the blessings and promises we have because of His grace, mercy, and love expressed to us. These encouraging remembrances effectively battle discouragement.

Resist
The third principle Nehemiah used in warring against discouragement was the call to resist: *"fight for your brothers, your sons, your daughters, your wives and your houses"* (v. 14). In the fight against discouragement, God's people are called to resist. We must not give in to fatigue, frustrations, failures, and fears. By not resisting and fighting your enemies (the old sinful flesh, the sinful world and the devil himself), you are already defeated along with your family. Learn how to fight this debilitating state called "discouragement" by reorganizing, remembering, and determining to fight (resist), by God's grace, until the task is done. James wrote, *"Submit therefore to God. Resist the devil and he will flee from you"* (James 4:7). Remember the devil is the author of discouragement. He uses our sinful tendencies to bend our thoughts away from right thinking, and tiredness will pave the way. When you resist him, you are resisting discouragement. Fix your mind on Christ and His Word. Remember that in His weariness as a man He was severely tested; He used Scripture to resist Satan, and so must you.

Discouragement is a choice. You can choose to allow despair to overshadow life or you can resist. Jeremy Taylor (1613-1667) once said, "It is impossible for that man to be discouraged who remembers that his Helper is omnipotent." The Apostle Paul wrote, *"We know that God causes all things to work together for good to those who love God, those who are called according to His purpose"* (Romans 8:28). That one verse removes a mountain of discouragement when a saint of the Lord grasps the truth of it, believes that truth, and thinks based on that truth. We have been provided with the best armor and weaponry by our Captain (Ephesians 6:10-18); use them and resist the enemies. Our life is lived in enemy country; be on the alert; keep your focus on your Lord and source of strength.

In His grace and providence He sends encouragement through others to us. Most Christians can recount that in times of trial and discouragement, the Lord most always has someone around who will give needed support or advice to get them back on track in their thinking. That someone may be a pastor, Sunday school teacher, wife, husband, or a Christian neighbor. Let me share a story that gives me support and perspective when my path seems dark and discouraging.

The story is told of a Union soldier, during the Civil War, who had fallen asleep while on guard duty. He was court-martialed and sentenced to death by a firing squad. Later it was discovered that he had mitigating circumstances which caused him to fall asleep; he had been on guard duty for more than 30 consecutive hours. It was decided that his death sentence should be commuted, but his commander had been killed in battle. Now the only person who had the authority to commute the sentence was the President of the United States, Abraham Lincoln. The soldier was given the necessary papers to take to Washington for the President to commute his death sentence. While traveling to the Capitol, the soldier was beaten and robbed of all his papers. Knowing the severity of his situation, the soldier continued making his way to the Capitol. Upon arriving at the White House, he discovered that he would not be allowed to see the President since he had no credentials validating who he was or why he was there.

Discouraged, the soldier sat down on a bench near the White House. In deep despair, with his head cradled in weary hands, he began to sob. A little boy was playing nearby and saw the soldier weeping. The boy walked over and asked the soldier why he was crying. The soldier responded by telling the boy that he should go away and not bother him. But the boy persisted until the soldier related his account of events to the lad. After hearing the story, the boy said in excitement, "Do you want to see the President? Come with me." Taking the soldier by the hand, the little boy led him to the front door of the White House. The guards at the entrance stepped back and opened the door for the boy and the soldier to pass through. Down through the hallways they walked until they came to the office door. Inside Abraham Lincoln, the President of the United States, was working. Still holding the hand of the soldier, the boy pushed the door open and brought the overwhelmed man right up to the desk of the great President, and little Tad Lincoln said,

"Daddy! This man needs to talk to you."

There was a day when I discovered, by God's grace, that I was under the just sentence of eternal death by a sovereign and holy God. I had no credentials to make me acceptable in His presence. Then God's Son came to me and escorted me into His presence where I found commute for my sentence of condemnation and death and forgiveness from the only One Who can forgive. Ever since then, when I find myself discouraged, I know I can go immediately into the very presence of God through His dear Son, who loved me and gave Himself for me; there I find every encouragement I need to face any issue or circumstance. You can too, if you are a child of God.

> *For we do not have a high priest who cannot sympathize with our weaknesses, but One who has been tempted in all things as we are, yet without sin.*

> *Therefore let us draw near with confidence to the throne of grace, so that we may receive grace to help in time of need.* (Hebrews 4:15-16).

---

1. Charles Spurgeon, Sermon #1069, Metropolitan Tabernacle Pulpit
2. Francis Schaeffer, *The Complete Works of Francis Schaeffer: A Christian Worldview, Volume 2, A Christian View of the Bible As Truth*, Crossway Books, 1982, p. 61
3. William Cowper, *To Mary* (written in the autumn of 1793, published by Hayley in 1803) written to and about the woman who cared for him for many years
4. Ravi Zacharias, *Let My People Think*, rzim.org

7

PORTRAITS OF DISCOURAGEMENT

Holy desperation is the door to God's greatest blessings.
Those who prove him best in the Scriptures were
at the end of everything. [1]

I will not be discouraged by failure;
I will not be elated by success. [2]

Trust in yourself and you are doomed to disappointment. [3]

Discouragement is dreaded and deadly when left unchecked. Dreaded because it is universal, recurring, and contagious, and deadly because it can quickly plunge its victim into a truly gloomy and dangerous part of DarkLand—depression.

Even when we are walking on the path which the Lord has placed before us, the uncertainty and difficulty which we will certainly encounter can tempt the Christian to think wrongly. If the light of His countenance is clouded over, the heart and mind cry out "I can't do this. Obeying God, not wavering, and following this perilous path is impossible!" At that point we may begin to mistrust our great King; if our spiritual eyes look around at the rubbish and difficulties instead of at Christ, we stray down the way of *discouragement* and *desperation* and *defeat*. Wrong thinking can quickly overwhelm. Be quick to run to the Savior in prayer and dependence. Always remember that adverse circumstances are intended to mold us, conform us, and drive us to trust our Lord. It is the dark, gloomy, and cloudy days, the trials in life, and the disappointments that are often used of the Lord to strengthen our faith. This is the reason James wrote, *"Consider it all joy, my brethren, when you encounter various trials, knowing that the testing of your faith produces endurance. And let endurance have its perfect result, so that you may be perfect and complete, lacking in nothing"* (James 1:2-4).

Emotions are God-given and discouragement is an emotion. But when Adam sinned, all the parts of mankind fell from perfection to corruption—even our emotions. The vessel which the Potter fashioned was spoiled and marred. Even so, the Lord can use discouragement; there are times when discouragement is used by God to move us, change us, and redirect us. Take for example the apostle Paul, who seems to express a form of discouragement when he had to suffer for the gospel's sake. He said:

> *We are afflicted in every way, but not crushed; perplexed, but not despairing; persecuted, but not forsaken; struck down, but not destroyed; always carrying about in the body the dying of Jesus, so that the life of Jesus also may be manifested in our body.* (2 Corinthians 4:8-10)

Paul did not allow discouragement to control him. Instead, he knew there was purpose, God's Purpose, in difficult and trying circumstances. The Apostle was not paralyzed and crushed by the adverse circumstances of persecution. As a child of God, if we can acknowledge and rest in the fact that there is a purpose in every situation, we can actually find light in the darkest of times. Christ is the Compass that always points true. No matter how hard, steep, or difficult the King's path may be at times, He has set markers, signs, and helps for us all along the way to steer us away from damaging or deadly detours that might lure Christians away from the Narrow Path with false promises of a path of ease. Even in the dark, the territory is still under the Lord's command and control. We can do what

James said, "*Consider it all joy...*" Do you see how your thinking about a circumstance can determine your emotions and actions or reactions?

Basically discouragement is *self-occupation*. When a person is discouraged, they are occupied with self and not others; they are evaluating circumstances in relationship to self. "What's happening to ME?" "MY plans are failing." What does it say about the human heart when the creature prefers his plans rather than the Creator's plan?

Discouragement is also looking at circumstances through the eyes of *self-ability*. If you really want to get discouraged, spend time examining all your inabilities and weaknesses; focus carefully on all the things that you CAN'T control. Too much of this will make you not want to get out of bed in the morning. Autopsies should be left to coroners!

The opposite of thinking in terms of self-occupation and self-ability is to think like Paul. *"I can do all things through Him who strengthens me"* (Philippians 4:13). Encouraging, don't you think? Do you really believe it? In ourselves we can do nothing, but in Him we can do all things including shaking off the shackles of discouragement. So the opposite of being self-centered, self-occupied, and depending on the failing ability of Self is to be Christocentric in our thinking. We are to think on His ability, His love, His promises, His power, His presence, and His willingness to save us. Christ Himself is our Encourager and our Power.

Remember the four reasons for discouragement: *Fatigue, Frustration, Failure,* and *Fear*. Remember the three treatments: *Reorganize, Remember,* and *Resist*. Now consider four men who were greatly loved and used by God: Moses, Elijah, Jonah, and Paul. They were servants, preachers, and prophets in His kingdom, yet they became discouraged and depressed to the point that three of them wanted the Lord to take their life. From these four men we can learn much about causes and cures for Discouragement. Perhaps we shall see ourselves in some way in each of these great servants of God.

Moses (Numbers 11)
Moses had been very successful in carrying out God's plan. He had been personally taught by the Lord on numerous occasions: in the desert, at the burning bush, the deliverance of Israel, the plagues upon Egypt, the parting of the Red Sea, the closing of the sea, and the miraculous feeding of the famished nation in the desert. No man had seen more and done more by God's power than had Moses. However, in Numbers 11 we find God's servant discouraged, defeated, despondent, depressed, and wanting God to take his life. *"So, if You are going to deal thus with me, please kill me at once, if I have found favor in Your sight, and do not let me see my wretchedness"* (Numbers 11:15).

What brought this great man of God to such a state of mind? As the appointed leader of the young nation Moses was assaulted by two specific blows.

First, the people that Moses led had not lost their appetite for the world; consequently they had *no heavenly appetite*.

> *The rabble who were among them had greedy desires; and also the sons of Israel wept again and said, "Who will give us meat to eat? We remember the fish which we used to eat freely in Egypt, the cucumbers and the melons and the leaks and the onions and the garlic, but now our appetite is gone. There is nothing at all to look at except this manna."* (Numbers 11:4-6)

Moses had been the instrument used of the Lord to deliver the children of Israel from under the bondage of the Egyptian Pharaoh. The Lord had miraculously brought them out through the Red Sea on their way to the land He had promised. God was protecting, providing, and feeding them with heavenly manna, but they lost their appetite for the bread from Heaven. Do you know anyone like these people? Have you seen people provided for and protected by the Lord, but they still have a worldly appetite and no appetite for the heavenly manna provided in the Lord Jesus Christ—worship, prayer, and Bible study? They would rather spend their time and money on earthly possessions, pleasures, and platitudes. It takes a heavenly appetite to feed on heavenly food.

The second thing that was pushing Moses toward the path of despair and discouragement was this: not only did the people not have an appetite for heavenly manna, but they were *complaining about the provisions of the Lord*. They looked back and craved the food of the world (Egypt); they were hungering for the cucumbers, melons, leaks, onions, and garlic of Egypt.

These two things would discourage any spiritual leader, but this was not what actually cast the dark shadow of discouragement over the mind of Moses. It was Moses' evaluation of the people's rebelling and complaining that plunged him into discouragement. His discouragement and desperation is clearly stated in Numbers 11:10-13.

> *Now Moses heard the people weeping throughout their families, each man at the doorway of his tent; and the anger of the LORD was kindled greatly, and Moses was displeased. So Moses said to the LORD, "Why have you been so hard on Your servant? And why have I not found favor in Your sight, that You have laid the burden of all this people on me? Was it*

> *I who conceived all this people? Was it I who brought them forth, that You should say to me, 'Carry them in your bosom as a nurse carries a nursing infant, to the land which You swore to their fathers'? Where am I to get meat to give to all this people? For they weep before me, saying, 'Give us meat that we may eat!'"*

It was Moses' *self-occupation* which led to his discouragement. Note in these verses his protests to God:

> "Why have you been so hard on your servant?"
> "Why have I not found favor in your sight?"
> "You have laid the burden of all this people on me."
> "Was it I who conceived all these people?"
> "Where am I to get meat to give to all this people?"

Notice how many times Moses uses "me" and "I." *Self-centeredness?* Moses is now occupied with Self, "Me" and "I." In other words, "Lord why are you treating me this way? I don't deserve all this."

Moses, the deliverer and leader, was fatigued, frustrated, felt like a failure, and was afraid. Why? The answer: *he was assuming responsibilities that did not belong to him.* The Lord did not assign to Moses the task of feeding and nurturing the people. Instead, it was the Lord who promised to care for them and take them into the Promised Land.

Moses was seeing every complaint of the people as a personal attack on himself. He assumed responsibilities the Lord had not given him, and he broke under the load. He said, *"I alone am not able to carry all this people, because it is too burdensome for me"* (Numbers 11:14).

When he looked at the needs of the people and then looked at his inability to provide them, discouragement and desperation came crushing in on him like a rockslide. Moses found himself in the shadowy territory of Giant Despair even though he had been an obedient servant of God. He now viewed everything in light of himself and his weaknesses. Fatigue, frustration, feelings of being a failure, and fear took his mind hostage and he became discouraged. When you or I take upon ourselves responsibilities which the Lord has not given us, our plight is going to be the same as that of Moses.

Observe the depth of Moses' discouragement. He actually asked God to take his life. *"So if You are going to deal thus with me, please kill me at once, if I have found favor in Your sight, and do not let me see my wretchedness"* (Numbers 11:15).

A paraphrase of this verse would read something like this: "Lord, if you are going to treat me this way, after all I have done for you, just kill me and put me out of my misery." He sat down and shook his shackles of despair.

In view of all this, what was God's solution? It should not surprise us to see that the first thing God did was to arrange a *reorganization* (Numbers 11:16-17).

> *The LORD therefore said to Moses, "Gather for Me seventy men from the elders of Israel, whom you know to be the elders of the people and their officers and bring them to the tent of meeting, and let them take their stand there with you. Then I will come down and speak with you there, and I will take of the Spirit who is upon you, and will put Him upon them; and they shall bear the burden of the people with you, so that you will not bear it all alone."*

He gave Moses seventy helpers and gifted them to stand with Moses and bear the burdens. The Lord also gave a promise for the encouragement of the people and for Moses; He Himself would provide meat to add to their diet of manna. *"Therefore the LORD will give you meat and you shall eat"* (Numbers 11:18).

We are not to take responsibilities which the Lord has not given us lest we become self-centered, fatigued, frustrated, feel like failures, and become fearful. These always lead to a state of discouragement and despair. It certainly happened to Moses.

> O LORD, I would delight in Thee,
> And on Thy care depend;
> To Thee in every trouble flee,
> My best, My only Friend.
> O that I had a stronger faith,
> To look within the veil;
> To credit what my Saviour saith,
> Whose words can never fail.
> He that has made my heaven secure
> Will here all good provide;
> While Christ is rich, I can't be poor;
> What can I want beside? [4]

Elijah (1 Kings 19)
Israel had followed after the false prophets and false gods of Jezebel. Elijah stood alone against King Ahab, Queen Jezebel, and all the false prophets of Baal. The climactic clash came at Mount Carmel.

> *So Ahab sent a message among all the sons of Israel and brought the prophets together at Mount Carmel. Elijah came near to all the people and said, "How long will you hesitate between two opinions? If the*

> *LORD is God, follow Him; but if Baal, follow him." But the people did not answer him a word.* (1 Kings 18:20-21)

The prophets of Baal called on their god all day without result; Elijah addressed God and fire came down from heaven.

> *"Answer me, O LORD, answer me, that this people may know that You, O LORD are God, and that You have turned their heart back again." Then the fire of the LORD fell and consumed the burnt offering and the wood and the stones and the dust, and licked up the water that was in the trench. When all the people saw it, they fell on their faces; and they said, "The LORD, He is God; the LORD, He is God." Then Elijah said to them, "Seize the prophets of Baal; do not let one of them escape." So they seized them; and Elijah brought them down to the brook Kishon, and slew them there.* (1 Kings 18:37-40)

With her prophets killed and her god disgraced Queen Jezebel was filled with rage. She gave Elijah 24 hours to get out of town.

> *Then Jezebel sent a messenger to Elijah, saying, "So may the gods do to me and even more, if I do not make your life as the life of one of them by tomorrow about this time." And he was afraid and arose and ran for his life and came to Beersheba, which belongs to Judah, and left his servant there. But he himself went a day's journey into the wilderness, and came and sat down under a juniper tree; and he requested for himself that he might die, and said, "It is*

enough; now, O LORD, take my life, for I am not better than my fathers." (1 Kings 19:2-4)

Fear struck Elijah and he ran; Discouragement was close behind. He was physically fatigued—emotionally frustrated—mentally a failure—and afraid for his life. He had become spiritually lax. Within a 24 hour period Elijah went from a mighty man of God, calling down fire on Baal's false prophets and killing them with a sword, to a man of doubts and fears, running for his life from a woman like a coward. He had become faint-hearted, spiritually careless, and desperately discouraged. Like Moses, he became so discouraged that he asked the Lord to take his life.

> O! I have seen the day,
> When, with a single word,
> God helping me to say,
> "My trust is in the Lord,"
> My soul has quelled a thousand foes,
> Fearless of all that could oppose.
> But unbelief, self-will,
> Self-righteousness, and pride,
> How often do they steal
> My weapon from my side! [5]

The first thing God did for Elijah in his discouraged state was to provide for his physical needs: a good night's sleep. (1 Kings 19: 5-8). If you're fatigued, a good night's sleep can do wonders for your mental outlook. How often are we burdened with a problem, tired from the activities of the day, and we lay down at night, but the problem doesn't go away; instead it enlarges, at least in our mind? We finally fall asleep, get a good night's rest, awake in the morning refreshed, and the problem we struggled with in the dark of night is much more manageable when day dawns.

The Lord then fed Elijah. A good night's sleep and a good nutritious meal can go a long way in helping us to think rightly. Drowsy eyes and an empty stomach are rarely able to fend off discouragement. It should go without saying that our diet has a great deal to do with how well we think. With a shaky hand and foggy lens the mind's telescope will never focus correctly; discouragement is inevitable. We need a clear mind and healthy body to cope with all the adverse circumstances in our lives; otherwise we stray from the right path and find ourselves on discouragement's road to despair.

Elijah had two good nights of sleep and plenty of food. Then it was time to get up! The angel of the LORD comes to him again. *"Arise, eat, because the journey is too great for you"* (1 Kings 19:7).

Elijah is instructed to go to *"Horeb, the mountain of God"* (1 Kings 19:8). He travels for forty days and forty nights; tired and sleepy, having not eaten or rested, Elijah stops in a cave and has another pity party.

> *Then he came there to a cave and lodged there; and behold, the word of the LORD came to him, and He said to him, "What are you doing here, Elijah?" He said, "I have been very zealous for the LORD, the God of hosts; for the sons of Israel have forsaken Your covenant, torn down Your altars and killed Your prophets with the sword. And I alone am left; and they seek my life, to take it away."* (1 Kings 19:9-10)

Finally Elijah is instructed to get off his "duff," quit feeling sorry for himself and do what the Lord called him to do (1 Kings 19:15-18). When he followed the instructions given him by the Lord, his discouragement fled like darkness from the rising sun.

Moses' discouragement came because he took upon himself responsibilities which God *had not given* him. The problem with Elijah was that he thought he was the only man God had, and he did not take the responsibility which God *had given* him. Both became self-centered, gave up, and wanted to die.

Jonah (Jonah 4)
Jonah saw a threat of defeat for his nation by the Assyrians. They dealt mercilessly with all nations and had badly treated Jonah's people, the people of Israel. Jonah had no love for the Assyrians. But God called Jonah to go to the capital of the Assyrian empire, Nineveh, and preach a warning message to the people of that pagan city. Jonah contemplated God's command, but decided to "take a cruise" instead—a cruise in the opposite direction of God's command. He purchased a ticket for passage on a boat sailing to Joppa. As you know, the Lord sent a fierce storm which resulted in Jonah being thrown overboard by the crew of the ship. He was swallowed by a fish, and remained in the stench and darkness of the fish's belly for three days and nights. After being brought to see things God's way, Jonah was vomited up on dry land. (Jonah 1).

These experiences brought Jonah to a state of willingness; willingness to do what the Lord told him to do at the very first. The Lord had his own way of getting Jonah to Nineveh, and to being willing to do exactly as instructed. God caused his prophet to do His bidding although Jonah had to go through a whale of an experience on his way to "willingness."

There are all kinds of instructions in God's word for every Christian. Tasks are before us; by the Holy Spirit we have been gifted to accomplish those tasks. Our duty may not be as difficult as was Jonah's, but is no less important. When we are engaged in serving Christ in work He has given, His peace is also given. Not doing those things which He has commissioned us to do will most likely bring difficulty and restlessness. There will be no peace in our heart and there will be no satisfaction in our lives: Discouragement!

Remember, trains are made to run on a track. When they are running on the track, they run smoothly and freely; when they jump the track they become nothing more than a pile of metal. Before they can become useful again they have to be picked up and put back on the track. Only then can the train do what it was constructed to do. The same is true with you and me. God created us to do certain things in our Christian life and he has given us the ability to accomplish the tasks He gives us. When we are doing those things we will be at peace, secure, and happy. But when we refuse to do what He tells us to do, we are disobedient; we've jumped the track. We'll become fatigued, frustrated, feel defeated and full of fear, then discouragement will settle in like a thick fog.

What does it take to bring us to God's way of thinking? Jonah, through an involuntary fish encounter, was put back on track. He became willing to do what God had commanded. He went to Nineveh with the simple message God had given: *"You have forty days to repent or God will destroy this city"* (Jonah 3:4). Shockingly, the people of that wicked city repented, including their king, and God spared them from judgment (Jonah 3:5-10). But the story isn't over.

Because of God's mercy to Nineveh, Jonah became angry, displeased with God for showing compassion to the people of that corrupt city. He wanted God's judgment to fall on them without mercy; after all, they were the enemy of Jonah's people, Israel (Jonah 4:1).

Jonah complains to God, trying to justify his initial rebellion. He says that he knew that if he preached to these people God would show mercy and that was the reason he rebelled (Jonah 4:2). No doubt these events created a fear in Jonah: a fear of going home to

Israel. Surely they would know what had transpired in Nineveh and would not look favorably on Jonah. The prophet had been the instrument for saving Nineveh and averting God's judgment.

A convergence of anger, resentment, and fear flowed into Jonah's heart, bringing fatigue, frustration, and a sense of failure and dread. He was self-centered and self-occupied; consequently, he became discouraged, which is reflected in his reaction. Jonah, a prophet of God, sat down and had a "poor me" party saying, *"Therefore now, O Lord, please take my life from me, for death is better to me than life"* (Jonah 4:3, 8). In other words, "Lord if you are going to treat the enemies of Israel in such a merciful way, just kill me and put me out of my misery. I don't agree with You!"

Jonah's big problem was that he didn't like the way God was running His business. He didn't comprehend how God could show mercy to the brutal enemies of God's own people, Israel. Jonah did not like or understand God's sovereignty in the affairs of men. This very issue is one with which people still struggle. The sovereignty of God is a big stumbling block for many people who don't like a God in charge, a God who accomplishes His purposes in history. Consequently, when He does something they don't like, similar to Jonah, men become angry, bitter, discouraged, and end up making foolish statements. You can't be angry with the Lord and expect to be happy and encouraged.

In each of these examples of discouraged men (Moses, Elijah, and Jonah), there is a common pattern: fatigue, frustration, sense of failure, and fear. Each of these men became so discouraged they wanted God to take their life. "Self" tried to usurp the throne; each man became self-occupied and self-centered. Everything became an issue of what will it do for or to ME, rather than what is God's will or purpose.

Moses took responsibilities which God had not given Him. Elijah thought he was the only one serving God and became cowardly and disobedient. Jonah did not like the way God was running His business. While each had a different problem, they ended up at the same place–self-occupied, self-centered, and desperately discouraged. Their discouragement led to an obvious state of depression. We will look at these men again in the next chapter where we discuss the subject of depression.

When discouragement comes to us, we need to stop, get some rest, and reorganize our thinking and actions. While we rest, we need to remember and rehearse in our mind all the blessings we enjoy because of the Person and Work of Christ. He lived a life we cannot live. He died a death we cannot die in order that we could be reconciled to God. He arose from the grave and ascended to the very throne of the universe to protect us and to provide all of our needs. He promises to take us home with Him when this life is ended. With rest, reorganization of our thoughts and actions, and remembrance of His promises, we can resist the assaults of Satan who ultimately wishes for us to live permanently in the dark fog and shadows of DarkLand.

> Be not discouraged; usefulness and trials, comforts and crosses, strength and exercise, go together. But remember He has said, "I will never leave thee, nor forsake thee; be thou faithful unto death, and I will give thee a crown of life." When you get to Heaven, you will not complain of the way by which the Lord brought you. [6]

The Apostle Paul (2 Corinthians 12)
It's hard to imagine anyone who suffered more for Christ than did the apostle Paul. From the time of his conversion on the road to Da-

mascus until he went to be with the Lord, Paul lived under the threat of suffering and peril of death. Read carefully, in his own writings, his catalogue of sufferings:

> *...in far more labors, in far more imprisonments, beaten times without number, often in danger of death. Five times I received from the Jews thirty-nine lashes. Three times I was beaten with rods, once I was stoned, three times I was shipwrecked, a night and a day I have spent in the deep. I have been on frequent journeys, in dangers from rivers, dangers from robbers, dangers from my countrymen, dangers from the Gentiles, dangers in the city, dangers in the wilderness, dangers on the sea, dangers among false brethren; I have been in labor and hardship, through many sleepless nights, in hunger and thirst, often without food, in cold and exposure.* (2 Corinthians 11:23-27)

In this same letter to the Corinthian church he says,

> *We are afflicted in every way, but not crushed; perplexed, but not despairing; persecuted, but not forsaken; struck down, but not destroyed; always carrying about in the body the dying of Jesus, so that the life of Jesus also may be manifested in our body. For we who live are constantly being delivered over to death for Jesus' sake, so that the life of Jesus also may be manifested in our mortal flesh.* (2 Corinthians 4:8-10)

If you were convinced that your difficult trials and circumstances were for the glory of Christ, as Paul did, would you not be less prone to discouragement? God says He is *"for us"* (Romans 8:31). Believe it! The King Himself has said it! With this view of life's circumstances, we could turn those things which often cause discouragement into a means of glorifying Christ. It is in the dark times of affliction that the world sees to whom we belong.

A little girl and her mother were traveling on a train several years ago. The little girl was playing and running up and down the isle of the train coach. Everyone was wondering who she belonged to. Suddenly the train entered a long tunnel and inside the coach it became pitch black darkness. When the train came out on the other side and daylight streamed through the windows, everyone knew who the little girl belonged to. She had fled to her mother in the darkness and was clinging to her with both arms.

When our Lord allows darkness to come upon us in our times of discouragement, all will know to Whom we belong, for we will flee to Him who loved us and gave Himself for us. Protection, encouragement, security, and peace are in His arms.

Trials of life can send us into an emotional tailspin resulting in discouragement, or those trials can be the instruments which give a clear testimony to the world that we are His, purchased by His own blood, and kept by His power. Note carefully the following prayer.

> Holy Father, Almighty God, We feel our weakness, our ignorance, our deep corruptions. We meekly knock at mercy's gate. Regard us in tender love—for Jesus' sake. Bend down Your ear- and grant Your smile. We are blind—be our light. We are steeped in selfishness—pluck all SELF out of us. In the deep sense of our guilt—we fly for refuge into the wounded side of Jesus! Be merciful, be merciful unto us—whose only hope is in Your unfailing mercy. Our sins rise higher

than the heavens—but Your merits in our behalf surpass the very heaven of heavens! Our unrighteousness would weight us down to hell—but Your glorious righteousness exalts us to Your heavenly throne! All things in us call for our damnation—but all things in You demand our forgiveness. We appeal, then, from Your throne of Perfect justice—to Your throne of boundless grace! Blessed Jesus, we hide ourselves in the sure covert of Your wrath-appeasing wounds! Grant us to hear Your voice assuring us: that by Your stripes we are healed; that You have been bruised for our iniquities; that You have been made sin for us—that we might have Your divine righteousness; and that all our vile and grievous iniquities, are forgiven and buried in the ocean of Your sin-concealing blood! We are guilty—yet pardoned! We are lost in ourselves—yet fully saved in You! Enable us to cling firmly to Your cross—even as we now seek safety and repose beneath its sin-atoning shelter! Let floods of sustaining grace from Your inexhaustible treasury, enrich our poor and weary souls. If the enemy approaches, quicken our steps to flee into the wounds of Jesus as our surer refuge! Sheltered in the ark of safety, may we cease to tremble at all alarms. May the good Shepherd lead us this day into the green pastures of His refreshing Word, and cause us to lie down beside the rivers of His divine comforts. These prayers we humbly offer in the name of Jesus Christ, and trusting only in His saving merits. Amen. [7]

1. Vance Havner, *Desperation*
2. J.B. Lightfoot (1828-1889)
3. D.L. Moody, from his biography, as quoted by dailychristianquotes.com
4. John Ryland, *Gadsby's Hymns*, William Gadsby (1773-1844), Hymn #247, Solid Ground Christian Books, 2009
5. William Cowper, *Olney Hymnal*, Book I, #17
6. John Newton, *Cardiphonia*, Morgan and Scott LD, 1911, p. 284
7. Henry Law (1797-1884), gracegems.org/g/ law_prayer_excerpts.htm

8

DEPRESSION

> You fearful saints fresh courage take,
> The clouds you so much dread,
> Are big with mercy and shall break
> In blessings on your head.
>
> Judge not the Lord by feeble sense,
> But trust Him for His grace;
> Behind a frowning providence
> He hides a smiling face. [1]

Depression (The Monster of DarkLand) has become one of the most well-known maladies of the human race; in fact, it has come to be called the common cold of Psychopathology. The range of opinions is vast; while I am not a physician who deals with depression medically, I have counseled with scores of people who claim to be or appear to be depressed. This chapter does not address depression from a medical standpoint but from the spiritual point of view. The Bible has a treasure-house of common sense instructions for Christians who are either troubled by depression or find themselves deep in the black depths and mazes of this part of DarkLand. Having said this, I do not dismiss the thought that there are cases where mood or mind altering drugs *may* be necessary. However, taking drugs for depression should be an absolute last resort and considered with great caution, being informed of side effects and long term consequences.

Volumes of information are now being published depicting and warning of the potential side effects of taking drugs for depression.

Among the many side effects are an increased risk of suicidal thinking and severe addiction. Studies exposing these dangers have forced the U.S. Food and Drug Administration (FDA) to require "Black Box" or "Black Label" warnings on the labels of mood altering prescription drugs. This warning means that medical studies indicate that the drug carries a significant risk of serious or even life-threatening adverse effects. According to the FDA, these dangers are especially relevant when these powerful drugs are prescribed for children or adolescents. This includes drugs prescribed for "ADHD" including *Ritalin, Concerta, Focalin, Methylin,* and *Metadate* and chemically similar amphetamines *Adderall* and *Dexedrine;* all are stimulants. (www.drugs.com/.../adhd-controversy-over-black-box-warning-1734)

In the previous chapter, I wrote that discouragement can be a forerunner of depression; three characteristics make discouragement a toxic problem: it is *universal*, it is *recurring*, and it is *contagious.* Is it not reasonable that if discouragement is the beginning of depression, then depression is rampant in our day because discouragement is rampant, unchecked, and unchallenged?

Also recall what has been stated concerning stress. Perhaps ours is the most stress laden culture that has ever existed; the ever changing and expanding technology which engulfs society worldwide exacerbates the stress. Since Stress is a great contributor to discouragement and is a part of depression, should we be surprised that there are so many despairing and depressed people? Small streams of stress can meet and form rivers of discouragement, which, in turn, if left to run freely, rush downward and empty out into a Lake of Despond and Depression where many people struggle in the stagnant and murky mire. And, as in John Bunyan's classic book *Pilgrim's Progress,* unless the Lord sends Help, rescue and escape are unlikely.

Thirty years ago I asked a pharmacist to give me the percentage of prescriptions being filled that were some form of an anti-depressant. The figure shocked me. It was 35%. That means that out of every three people who are taking prescription drugs, one of them are taking some form of anti-depressants. If there were 35% of the people taking some kind of mood altering drug 30 years ago, what do you think that percentage is today? Statistics paint a portrait, and that portrait of society is a sad and gloomy one.

Sometimes it seems that the medical profession looks at depression as if it were a new problem, but the truth is depression has been around since the fall of man in the Garden of Eden. In ancient times it was called *melancholia* but the symptoms were the same—sadness, sleeplessness, discouraged hopeless feelings, etc. Depression is not new nor should it surprise us that sinful men become depressed. In many cases the symptoms of depression spring from sinful actions, whether doing something we shouldn't do, or not doing what we should do. The following is a partial list of "symptoms."

> Feelings of hopelessness and pessimism.
> Feelings of worthlessness, helplessness, and guilt.
> Loss of interest in things you once enjoyed, including sex.
> Struggling to concentrate, remember, and make decisions.
> Loss of energy, fatigue, fear, and frustration.
> Loss of appetite and weight loss, or overeating and weight gain.
> Insomnia or oversleeping.
> Thoughts of death and suicide, attempted suicide.
> Restlessness and irritability.

These are but a few of the so-called symptoms of depression. There are times when each of us may experience one or more of these symptoms, but are not in reality "depressed." Depression's roots grow deep and its fruit hangs rotting and heavy on the soul. Depression is not fleeting, but lingering and clinging. A truly depressed person sees life as if looking through a cracked lens which distorts and deceives the mind. In this part of DarkLand the fog is so heavy and oppressive that those who find themselves there perceive no hope of relief or escape. Sadly people around them are affected also.

You have already read about some of the Bible heroes who were discouraged and stressed; some became depressed such as Moses, Elijah, and Jonah. Some of the giants in Christian history were men who often found themselves thrust into this dark country. Depression plagued Charles Spurgeon, John Calvin, Martin Luther, William Cowper, Richard Baxter, and D.L. Moody, just to name a few. No one is exempt; this wolf hunts all of God's sheep. If you do not handle stress and discouragement scripturally, you may find yourself being swept toward the mire and perilous Territory of Depression.

Examples are often the best of teachers. I want to use two biblical characters to help us think and reason scripturally concerning this enemy of the mind. To better understand depression, it's beneficial to analyze the life of someone who was depressed. Although these men and their situations have been discussed in chapters six and seven on Discouragement, I want to go further. Some thoughts used in discouragement may be repeated because there is only a very fine line between discouragement and depression, and many things which describe discouragement have common characteristics in a discussion of depression. Both Moses and Elijah are portraits of discouragement and depression. Their stories are scriptural illustrations of the signs and causes of depression. From Scripture, learn how God dealt with their depression.

Moses and Depression
Moses was a man swept into the dark distorted heart of DarkLand that is depression. Recall his story as discussed in the previous chap-

ter and how events and people brought discouragement into his life. But discouragement is a wicked deceiver that draws its target toward more dark and wrong thinking. Does Scripture confirm that? Examine the symptoms which Moses experienced as recorded in Numbers 11:11-15.

> So Moses said to the LORD, "Why have You been so hard on Your servant? And why have I not found favor in Your sight, that You have laid the burden of all this people on me? Was it I who conceived all this people? Was it I who brought them forth, that You should say to me, 'Carry them in your bosom as a nurse carries a nursing infant, to the land which You swore to their fathers'? Where am I to get meat to give to all this people? For they weep before me, saying, 'Give us meat that we may eat!' I alone am not able to carry all this people, because it is too burdensome for me. So if You are going to deal thus with me, please kill me at once, if I have found favor in Your sight, and do not let me see my wretchedness."

Moses *lost hope*; he *wanted to die*.
He *lost perspective* on life and his mission. He thought there was *no way out*.
He wanted to *withdraw*; he *wanted out* of this mess.
He was *angry*: "Where am I going to get food to feed these people, I didn't bring them into the world?"
He *felt like a failure*.

There they are, warning signs of depression: lost hope, wanting to die, loss of perspective on life, seeing no way out, wanting to withdraw, anger, and feeling like a failure. Stress and discouragement swept Moses into the foggy and fearful world of Depression; he saw no solution or escape. He had seen God perform astounding acts of power and deliverance in the past, but Moses, the servant of God, was now viewing everything through severely "cracked lenses" and everything was distorted; Moses wanted to die. What caused this to happen to such a man as Moses?

What factors play such strong roles in drawing the mind past discouragement and into the darkest of blackness—Depression? There are common contributors many of which are also overlapping symptoms of discouragement; this should not be a surprise since discouragement can be the gateway to Depression.

> Experiencing a loss through death, divorce, loss of job, loss of health
> Poor diet
> Not enough sleep/rest
> Repressed anger
> Reactions to drugs, or between drugs (prescription drugs as well as non-prescription)
> Physical ailments: hypoglycemia, infections associated with the brain or nervous system, general body infections, hepatitis, hormonal irregularities, etc. (if this is you, see a physician)
> Physical exhaustion—overdoing good things
> Guilt

While all these are important to consider, I believe the most common cause of depression is *faulty thinking*. This was Moses' problem, although some of the above contributors were also present. Except for clear-cut diagnosable organic medical problems, most all in the list above lead to discouragement and often descend into depression through *faulty thinking*. How you react to a particular circumstance is determined by how you think about that circumstance. I mentioned this in the previous chapter dealing with discouragement. It is important, so let me repeat it: HOW YOU REACT TO A PARTICULAR CIRCUMSTANCE IS DETERMINED BY HOW YOU THINK ABOUT THAT CIRCUMSTANCE. Follow this process. You are faced with a circumstance, then you begin to evaluate (think about) that circumstance. The way you think about it will determine your emotions, and out of your emotions you will act or react. Here is the word picture:

Circumstance >>>> Thinking >>>> Emotions >>>> Reaction

If you want to change your emotions, actions, and reactions you will have to change how you think. Evaluation determines actions or re-action. Think negatively and you will react negatively; then distress, discouragement, and depression are ready to draw the Christian further down a wrong and unsafe path. We must think and evaluate using the light of God's Truth. Jesus said, *"You will know the truth and the truth will make you free"* (John 8:32). It is not the truth in and of itself that makes you free, but the knowledge of the truth; that knowledge will contribute to right thinking. Suppose the truth is that flood waters have washed out a bridge on a road on which I am traveling. It is night and I don't know the bridge is out. Most likely I will drive into the rushing waters and drown. The truth did not change because I did not know the bridge was out. But if I had known the truth, I would not have plunged headlong into disaster.

Persistent *faulty thinking* unites stress and discouragement into a rushing surge which, left unchecked by Truth, will only stop when it plunges its victim mercilessly into the Lake of *Despair* and *Depression*. This is one of DarkLand's deadliest places where all seems lost, hopeless, and without purpose. There are three areas within a *faulty thinking* process that may lead us to this miserable state. First, there is the process of ***devaluing self:***

"I'm useless and broken."
"I make a mess of everything I try to do."
"I'm a hopeless failure."

As a Christian, we should never think in those terms. We are blood-bought at great cost by the Lord Jesus Christ; what has cost God so much should never be thought of lightly by us. We are in the family of God. We are children of God. We are precious to Him. We are heirs with and in Christ. He has a purpose for each of us and He will accomplish that purpose in our lives. We must look to Christ and not at ourselves. Looking at the holes in a screen door won't keep the flies out, but taking the old screen out and replacing it with a new one will—so it is with our thinking. We will have to replace old *faulty thinking*, which is full of holes, with *scriptural thinking* about self.

A second area of faulty thinking is ***unscriptural evaluation of a situation***; its effects on me will always cause stress and a compounding of problems—often expressed in such comments as:

"It's all over for me."
"My life is a waste."
"There is no way out of the mess I'm in."
"This is a hopeless situation no matter what I do."
"God has abandoned me."
"No matter how much I pray nothing happens."

Again, this is *evaluating a circumstance* based on our own human analysis and abilities rather than looking to Christ who is our Wisdom, Compass, Anchor, Strength: He is whatever we need. Paul said, *"I can do all things through Christ who strengthens me"* (Philippians 4:13). He did not face the issues of life in His own strength, *"I know whom I have believed and am convinced that He is able to* guard what I have entrusted to Him until that day" (2 Timothy 1:12).

> For the most part, God's people are exercised with sharp trials and temptations; for it is necessary they should learn not only what He can do for them—but how little they can do without Him! [2]

A third part of *faulty thinking* which will lead to despair and depression is **wrong thinking in regard to the future.** Some of those thoughts go something like this:

> "I'll never make it."
> "I will never amount to anything, life is hopeless for me."
> "Will my children care for me when I'm sick?"
> "What will I live on when I'm old?"
> "Will God abandon me forever?"

For Christians, our lives and futures are in the hands of our loving and compassionate Lord. Since we have been brought to faith in Christ we are His children and are His responsibility. Our future is settled, *"For those whom He foreknew, He also predestined to become conformed to the image of His Son..."* (Romans 8:29). As Christians, our destiny is purposed and assured; that future is not negative. Our great Lord never gets distracted; He never forgets His business; He never loses sheep.

> We are to trust His heart—when we cannot see His hand! We are to believe Him—when we cannot understand His mysterious workings!
>
> Beloved, is God cleansing you by fiery trials, or causing you to pass through deep waters? Are you at

> a loss to know what His design is, or where the present affliction will end?
>
> Be still. Wait His time. There is a divine **working** time—which is the present; and there is a divine **revealing** time—which is to come.
>
> The wisest Christians are often in the dark now—but the simplest Christians will see all things clearly by and by. [3]

These three areas of *faulty thinking*—devaluating self, unscriptural evaluation of circumstances, and wrong thinking in regard to the future—fall under the umbrella of "worry"; and worry is a state of mistrust and sin. When you're worried, you are not trusting in the Lord for "the beginning of anxiety is the end of faith. The beginning of true faith is the end of anxiety." [4]

I heard the late and highly respected preacher, Vance Havner, say in a sermon, "Worry, is like a rocking chair, it will give you something to do, but it won't get you anywhere."

My wife and I love to watch the birds in our yard. A lot can be learned by observing God's creatures. Have you ever noticed how the Lord feeds the birds? Birds don't worry about having a better nest than their neighbors or having more nests than their neighbor? Have you ever seen a dog worried because he doesn't have enough bones buried to provide for his old age? I doubt that squirrels worry about having enough nuts stored beyond the upcoming winter (Matthew 6:25-34).

Each of these areas of *faulty thinking* is negative: *devaluing self, unscriptural evaluation of a given situation*, and *wrong thinking in re-*

gard to the future. This was Moses' sin and it was also Elijah's. Faulty thinking escorted Elijah into discouragement, then deep into DarkLand, down to the Valley of Depression and Mire of Despair.

Elijah: Depression's Faulty Thinking
You should remember that Elijah was a mighty prophet, a spokesman of God to Israel for several years. During that period he was fearless, but a woman's threats sent him running scared to the desert. The account in 1 Kings 19 recounts the prophet's plunge into the vortex of depression.

> *"And he [Elijah] was afraid and arose and ran for his life and came to Beersheba, which belongs to Judah, and left his servant there. But he himself went a day's journey into the wilderness, and came and sat down under a juniper tree; and he requested for himself that he might die, and said, "It is enough; now, O LORD, take my life, for I am not better than my fathers."* (1 Kings 19:3-4)

He became physically tired, emotionally exhausted, spiritually lax, hungry, feeling guilty, lonely, resentful, and feared for his life. There is no question, Elijah was depressed and wanted to die.

Want to know an interesting fact about Elijah? *"Elijah was a man with a nature like ours..."* (James 5:17). Elijah was subject to depression and so are you. His sin was Faulty Thinking.

1. Elijah focused on feeling and not fact. He was afraid and ran for his life. He sat under a juniper tree and wished to die. "Lord, I've had enough. I'm fed up. I don't want any more of this." He *felt* like a failure and a coward. No doubt guilt arose within him for having those feelings After all the mighty works the Lord had done through him, now Elijah couldn't find it in himself to trust God, and that state added to his misery and faulty thinking.

The prophet was thinking and reasoning based on emotion which can be destructive! Thinking that something *is* true simply because you *feel* that it's true is dangerous. In his mind, feelings equaled truth. We must learn and trust that feelings are not necessarily fact. Feelings are highly unreliable. What would happen if you told your spouse that you didn't *feel* married anymore? You'd probably get a good lecture on feelings vs. facts!

The great Reformer Martin Luther wrote the following poem concerning feelings.

> Feelings come and feelings go,
> And feelings are deceiving;
> My warrant is the Word of God—
> Naught else is worth believing.
>
> Though all my heart should feel condemned
> For want of some sweet token,
> There is One greater than my heart
> Whose Word cannot be broken.
>
> I'll trust in God's unchanging Word
> Till soul and body sever,
> For though all things shall pass away,
> His Word shall last forever!

You cannot trust feelings. Evaluate with truth and trust so that depression will have no place to take root in your life. Jesus said, *"you will know the truth and the truth will make you free"* (John 8:32). When you direct your mind away from self and to Christ Himself and His work, and remember that circumstances are either caused or allowed by the sovereign Lord for your good and His glory, then your thinking will be scriptural and true, bringing clarity and encouragement, not discouragement and depression.

Romans 8:28 is not in the Bible to take up space, but is written for your instruction, encouragement, and strength. When you come to recognize that God is sovereign and does things according to the counsel of His own will (Ephesians 1:11), then you can trust Him in any situation. This is a hard lesson for us to learn because we want to be in control and know what is going on and why. But the child of God is not his own, he has been purchased: *"For you have been bought with a price: therefore glorify God in your body..."* (1 Corinthians 6:20). If you belong to Him, you are not in control, He is! You must surrender to His will in all circumstances. If we think correctly, we will not become depressed over the issues of life.

Remember, in every circumstance God is preaching a sermon to you. Don't focus on your feelings, but seek, through prayer, the truth in those circumstances. You may not always get an immediate answer, but you will get an answer. This is one of the great privileges of the Christian. Unbelievers do not have this privilege. Unbelievers have a valid reason to be depressed. They face problems with nothing more than their own limited understanding and lack of strength; despair and depression lay in wait in every part of their lives. Those who turn away from God rarely consider what they're turning to.

2. Elijah compared himself to others (v. 4). How easy it is to compare ourselves with others. "O! If I could just have faith like ..." This may be a universal practice, but it is faulty thinking. Listen to what Paul said, *"For we are not bold to class or compare ourselves with some of those who commend themselves; but when they measure themselves by themselves and compare themselves with themselves, they are without understanding"* (2 Corinthians 10:12).

It would be foolish to think that God makes people identical, giving them the same personality, temperament, gifts, or missions. There is only one person who can be *you* and that's *you*. When you compare yourself to others you compare your weaknesses to their strengths, in which case you'll always come up short. This kind of comparison and thinking can lead to discouragement and depression. You will be caught in the prison of "I should." "I should be like that person"; or "I should be able to do what that person does"; "my family should be like theirs," etc. Come to think of it, that kind of thinking is kind of depressing all by itself, isn't it? Author, playwright, and poet Oscar Wilde said, "Be yourself—everyone else is already taken."

You must guard against the opposite also, which is thinking that you are over, better, and above everyone else. A braggart is full of conceit and pride and headed for a fall. If a true Christian has the tendency to be a braggart, he would do well to humble himself, or he will *be humbled* by the Lord.

3. *Falsely blaming self.* Read what Elijah said to God in 1 Kings 19:10:

> *I have been very zealous for the LORD, the God of hosts; for the sons of Israel have forsaken Your covenant, torn down Your altars and killed Your prophets with the sword. And I alone am left; and they seek my life, to take it away.*

In effect, God's prophet was saying, "Lord I have worked for three years, but I see no change in the people. What have I done wrong?" He was falsely blaming himself for events and circumstances. Such thinking quickly wounds us and pulls us toward depression. When you assume a responsibility that God never gave you, as did Moses and Elijah, it will always be more of a load than you can carry. You cannot take the blame for other people's responses when you minister to them. It is not your job to be *successful* in ministering, but it is your job to be *faithful* in ministering to people. In speaking of our responsibility to witness or tell people the gospel, I heard Vance Havner say, "It's not my job to see that they like it, but it is my job to see that they get it."

I see this quite often in parents whose children have gotten into trouble. If the parent has sought to be biblically rearing their child in the *"nurture and admonition of the Lord"* (Ephesians 6:4), then they should not blame themselves for the erring child. They certainly should be burdened and concerned for the salvation and spiritual condition of their children, but blaming self can be very depressing. I must hasten to add that there are times when the parents *have* failed to rear their children in the nurture and admonition of the Lord and their children's present activities are directly traceable back to the teaching (or lack thereof) and examples given by their parents. This calls for repentance, prayer, and wisdom from Christ.

I have met people who are always negative about themselves. Consequently, every event in their life is weighed by a negative analysis. "I knew this was going to happen, it always happens to me." "Nothing good ever comes my way." This is a person who is probably depressed in some degree most of the time.

A child of God should never fall into the trap of always blaming self. Certainly there are some things in life we must justly take the blame for, but we do not brood ourselves into depression because of it. We go to the Lord confessing our sins, receive His forgiveness and move on to correct the problem if we can.

4. Elijah exaggerated the negative. "Lord, I have remained faithful to you and all these other fellows have *'forsaken your covenant, torn down your altars and killed Your prophets with the sword. And I alone am left; and they seek my life to take it away'"* (1 Kings 19:10).

Elijah was really saying, "Lord I am the only faithful one left"; a mixture of self-pity, arrogance, and self-exaltation. Again, this was *feeling* not *fact*. Elijah concluded that everyone was against him and was trying to take his life.

5. Elijah's actions were acts of disobedience to God. Disobedience is a major root of depression. If we are not thinking properly we will be acting improperly—disobedient. The Bible clearly instructs us, *"Be anxious (worrying) for nothing, but in everything by prayer and supplication with thanksgiving let your requests be made know to God. And the peace of God, which surpasses all comprehension, will guard your hearts and your minds in Christ Jesus."* (Philippians 4:6-7). We are commanded to pray and trust. Where there are fears and worries, they are usually preceded by lack of prayer and faith in Christ; in that disobedience wrong thinking finds fertile ground to take root. Both prayer and faith seem to be absent in the life of Elijah at this time. Weak in prayer, weak in everything.

If he had logically analyzed what he was thinking, he would have realized that if Jezebel wanted to kill him, she would not have sent a messenger to warn him. The fact was, Jezebel could not afford to have him killed because of his popularity with the people. He would have become a martyr; Jezebel knew that.

Elijah was not thinking with his mind, he was responding with his emotions; consequently the negative was exaggerated. He was not the only faithful person. God set him straight in 1 Kings 19:18: *"Yet I will leave 7000 in Israel, all the knees have not bowed to Baal and every mouth that has not kissed him."* When we feel sorry for ourselves and dwell on the negative, we will likewise become depressed. I have asked this question earlier, but I want to ask it again, have you ever gone to bed with a big problem on your mind? You wrestled and wrestled until you finally fell asleep. You dwelt on the negative and the problem grew and grew. When you awakened the next morning and began to think clearly, you discovered that the problem was not quite as big as it seemed to be the night before.

When we dwell on the negative we exaggerate it and the weight becomes heavier and heavier to bear. Depression draws us in and the problem begins to control us.

Elijah's faulty thinking led Him into a state of severe depression. What was God's prescription for healing His prophet?

God's Remedy for Elijah's Depression
1. Take care of the physical first (1 Kings 19:5-8). God gave him rest and food which lasted for 40 days. Good sleep and a good breakfast can go a long way in bringing sunshine into a person's life instead of a day of dark clouds and gloom.

Notice, God did not rebuke Elijah by saying something like, "You coward, what are you doing here? Did I not show you what I can do?" Instead of a rebuke, God tenderly and lovingly addressed and provided his needs, just like a good shepherd cares for an injured or tired lamb. When a person is depressed, they need love and not a judgmental attitude. If the stomach is hungry and the body weak or distraught, the mind doesn't think clearly. Physical and personal needs that have worn down a person to a point of depression may also include loss of a job, a car for transportation, a place to live, or even food. Examine and take care of the physical first if you want to help a depressed fellow Christian. Once the physical is cared for, then comes the encouragements and reminders of the great and sure promises of God. This principle also applies in witnessing to the lost.

If *you* are a Christian and depressed, the place to start is with a close look at the physical; have a good medical examination, get some rest and relaxation, exercise, and eat a good balanced diet. Take care of the physical first in order to restore right thinking.

2. Surrender to the Lord those things that are frustrating you; those things which you have not been able to control or conquer. It's amazing to me to see how the Lord allowed Elijah to unload his frustrations, even though Elijah was wrong and sinful in the way he acted and in what he said (1 Kings 19:9-10).

Elijah had fled to a cave and was hiding, but the Lord came to him. God spoke with a question first: *"What are you doing here, Elijah?"* (1 Kings 19:9). The question was not for God's information. He asked the question to allow Elijah to articulate what was in his mind. We see the Lord doing the same thing with Job in the book of Job. Is it not amazing grace, mercy, and love when the Lord allows us to vent our frustrations, fears, disappointments, failures, insecurities, and doubts, so that He can correct our thinking and encourage us? Note the six emotions Elijah felt; all result in improper thinking—sinful thinking.

> Fear (1 Kings 19:3).
> Resentment (1 Kings 19:4).
> Lack of confidence, no better than others (1 Kings 19:4).
> Anger (1 Kings 19:10)—he had worked hard for nothing.
> Loneliness (1 Kings 19:10)—"I'm all alone."
> Paranoia (worry), "They want to kill me." (1 Kings 19:10)

In the same manner, Moses, Job, and Jonah fell into the same state of mind as did Elijah; they all vented their frustrations to the Lord. If you're depressed, you need to communicate your problems to the Lord as did those great men. We generally deal with our frustrations in either of two wrong ways, namely, *ventilation* (blowing up and lashing out in anger), or *internalization* (repressing feelings and anger); neither is scriptural and both can draw the mind into distorted thinking and to depression. Take frustrations and failings to the Lord.

> Lord, I cannot let Thee go,
> Till a blessing Thou bestow;
> Do not turn away Thy face;
> Mine's an urgent, pressing case.
>
> Thou didst once a wretch behold,
> In rebellion blindly bold;
> Scorn Thy grace; Thy power defy;
> That poor rebel, Lord, was I.
>
> Once a sinner near despair
> Sought Thy mercy-seat by prayer;
> Mercy heard and set him free;
> Lord, that mercy came to me.
>
> Many days have passed since then;
> Many changes I have seen;
> Yet have been upheld till now;
> Who could hold me up but Thou?
>
> Thou hast helped in every need;
> This emboldens me to plead;
> After so much mercy past,
> Canst Thou let me sink at last?
>
> No; I must maintain my hold;
> 'Tis Thy goodness makes me bold;
> I can no denial take,
> When I plead for Jesus' sake. [5]

3. Renew your awareness of the Lord's presence (1 Kings 19:11-13). Although the Lord sent the wind, the earthquake, and the fire, His personal and conscious Presence was not known to Elijah in those things. His Presence was known when He spoke to Elijah in a gentle whisper—not in the fury and might of wind, earthquake, or fire. If we find ourselves in the blackness of depression, we need to be alone with the Lord, crying out to Him and expressing our doubts, fears, frustrations—everything! Then wait; be silent; listen for Him to speak. You will never renew your awareness of the presence of the Lord until you are willing to spend time in reading His word, voicing your problems to Him in prayer, and meditating on His glory and promises.

> *If any of you lacks wisdom, let him ask of God, who gives to all generously and without reproach, and it will be given him. But he must ask in faith without any doubting, for the one who doubts is like the surf of the sea, driven and tossed by the wind.* (James 1:5-6)

4. Follow His directions for your life (1 Kings 19:15). Do you remember the illustration of the train jumping the track? Elijah had jumped the track and now the Lord is putting Him back on track. Elijah received his assignment. God put Elijah back to work. The quickest way to defeat depression is O B E D I E N C E—doing what the Lord tells you to do.

Following these four actions will lead to right and positive thinking. When you see that the Lord has a purpose for you and your life, then you will no longer see yourself as a failure, beyond help, and forsaken. *"You shall know the truth and the truth will make you free"* (John 8:32). The more Truth you know the more freedom you will experience. Depression is bondage in the worst possible dungeon in the worst possible part of DarkLand; and the chains and iron gates of that dungeon are fashioned and given strength by improper unscriptural thinking—sinful thinking!

The mistakes which lead so often to depression are: focusing on feeling not fact, comparing oneself to others, falsely blaming self for perceived failures, and exaggerating the negative. God's remedy for Elijah's depression was caring for the physical first, turning his frustrations over to the Lord, renewing his awareness of the presence of the Lord, and following the Lord's directions. You have tried everything else; why not try the Lord's prescription?

Remember all the stormy seas around you cannot sink your ship unless you punch holes in your mind by improper thinking. The storm and raging sea would have never bothered Peter when he was walking on the water had he not taken his eyes off of Christ and began to gaze at the storm and raging waves around him (Matthew 14:30).

In his autobiography Martin Luther says, "I have one preacher I love better than any other; it is my little tame robin, who preaches to me daily. I put his crumbs upon my window sill, especially at night. He hops onto the sill when his supply is there, and takes as much as he desires to satisfy his need. From thence he always hops to a little tree close by, and lifts up his voice to God, and sings his carol of praise and gratitude, tucks his little head under his wings, and goes fast to sleep, to leave tomorrow to look after itself."

> My soul is sad and much dismayed;
> See Lord what legions of my foes,
> With fierce Apollyon at the head,
> My heavenly pilgrimage oppose!
>
> Their fierce arrows reach their mark,
> My throbbing heart with anguish tear;

Each lights upon a kindred spark,
And finds abundant fuel there.

Come then and chase the cruel host,
Heal the deep wounds I have received!
Nor let the powers of darkness boast,
That I am soiled and Thou art grieved! [6]

---

1 William Cowper, *Olney Hymnal*, Book III, Hymn #15, 1797
2 John Newton, gracegems.org/newton/additional_letters_of_newton.html
3 James Smith (1802-1862), gracegems.org
4 George Mueller (1805-1898), dailychristianquotes.com
5 John Newton, *Olney Hymnal*, Book I, #10
6 William Cowper, *Olney Hymnal*, Book III, #20

9

IMPATIENCE

Impatience is a misunderstanding of the Providence of God.

I love the little prayer that goes something like this: "Lord, make me more patient and do it now!" That little prayer describes our generation very well.

If we were to take a poll, most of us would mark *patience* as one of our most difficult spiritual assignments and *impatience* as one of the great contributors to our discomfort and anxieties. Our efforts and aspirations to develop a patient character are increasingly complicated by the fact that almost everything around us is "instant." We have fast food restaurants, instant entertainment on our televisions, instant information on our computers, instant communication on our smart phones, and even drive-through funeral homes. The world we live in is a "Happening Now" world and the United States is the country of "Mount Rush More." We're like butterflies flitting from one flower to another. Waiting is a lost virtue. We can get in our automobiles and drive to a restaurant, order a meal from the car, pick it up at a drive-thru window, take it home, turn on our television, eat our supper, and watch most of the major events that took place in the world on that particular day. And we can probably do it all in one hour.

The big question is, "What is all this doing to our spiritual life?" Take a little test with me and you can grade yourself with the following questions.

1. How do you respond when the car in front of you doesn't move immediately when the traffic light turns green?

2. What are your reactions when you get in the checkout line at a store and there is a very slow cashier, or an older lady has trouble finding her change or check book?

3. How long does it take you to become agitated when you have a long wait, well beyond your appointment time, at the doctor's office?

4. Do you have anger toward the Lord when you are watching a loved one suffer with a terminal disease?

5. How do you react at your favorite restaurant to someone's unruly children sitting nearby?

How did you do on the test? Do you see how impatient you really are?

Impatience has Consequences
Waiting can be very challenging and frustrating to us, but God is in no hurry. He does not alter His plans and purposes one iota to accommodate an impatient and restless generation or individual. Not only is waiting frustrating for us, but it sometimes opens doors for Satan's attacks, as was the case with Abraham and Sarah. Impatience is an open door for the Devil to cause tremendous suffering. Impatience can be dangerous. An old Chinese proverb says: "One moment of patience may ward off great disaster. One moment of impatience may ruin a whole life."

God had promised Abraham (Genesis 15) that he would have an heir and descendants as numerous as the stars. But as they grew old Sarah and Abraham became impatient and unwilling to wait for the Lord to fulfill His promise to them. They decided to take over; the result—an illegitimate child, Ishmael, and terrible, far-reaching family problems. God never blessed their actions. Consequences of Abraham and Sarah's impatience have marched through history all the way down to our day. The same pattern in their impatience can be seen in the lives of men and women today. There were four movements to their impatience.

First, a promise was given to them. Their impatience was directly related to expectation based on the promise of God. When the expected does not occur, impatience raises its ugly Medusa head. The more important one values a promise, the higher the expectation, and the greater will be the temptation to become impatient.

God promised Abraham a son (Genesis 15:4-6) and this promise was extremely important to Abraham. In his day to be without a child, especially a male child, was cause for shame and humiliation. Abraham's pride was at stake, "What will people think if I have no son?" Consequently, the expectation was especially high, which intensified the impatience.

Remember also that this promised son would be important to God's purpose in the Messianic promise. As far as Satan knew, the child promised to Abraham and Sarah might be the Messiah. Satan capitalizes on Sarah's impatience, enticing her to consider a substitute son in the house of Abraham. You can almost hear the echo of Satan's word to Eve when he put doubt in Eve's mind concerning God's words, *"Indeed, has God said...?"* (Genesis 3:1). In her impatience Sarah convinces Abraham to father an illegitimate child with Hagar, Sarah's Egyptian handmaid. We should never underestimate the ability of Satan to take advantage of our impatience in efforts to thwart God's purpose and to destroy us.

God has given us a book of promises, the Bible, and this book assures us of God's providential protection, His presence, His perseverance or patience with us, and our ultimate victory over the circumstances that come to us. He has promised. *"And we know that God causes all things to work together for good to those who love God, to those who are called according to His purpose"* (Romans 8:28). But when we actually go through difficult and hard-to-understand circumstances we may find ourselves thinking, "WHEN is He going to fulfill that promise?" "IS He going to keep His Word?" IMPATIENCE! True faith in the Lord waits and trusts until He is ready to fulfill His word. How well are you waiting upon the Lord?

> *Yet those who wait for the LORD will gain new strength; They will mount up with wings like eagles, They will run and not get tired, They will walk and not become weary.* (Isaiah 40:31)

Second, Impatience is associated with perceived possibility or impossibility. We tend to become impatient with the Lord when His promises are *perceived* to be unlikely or impossible. When this occurs in our thinking process, we assume that we must work out our own problems; give God a little help. *"So Sarah said to Abram, 'Now behold the Lord has prevented me from bearing children. Please go in to my maid; perhaps I will obtain children through her.' And Abram listened to the voice of his wife"* (Genesis 16:2). Since the promise of a child had not been fulfilled and since she thought she was too old to have a child, Sarah concluded that the Lord needed some help, so she talked Abram into taking a surrogate, Hagar, and fathering a child by her. Sarah's problem was a lack of faith. She had forgotten how great God is (Genesis 18:9-15). She thought God had made a promise that He would not or could not keep. She felt that she had waited long enough, so she took matters into her own hands.

Third, Impatience is associated with God's plans. Sarah was a modern day thinker. To some extent, she reasoned that God helps those who help themselves. Rather than patiently waiting upon the Lord for the fulfillment of His plan, she concocted her own plan. Hagar did conceive and bore a son—Ishmael. Abraham loved Ishmael and wanted him to be the promised son (Genesis 17:18).

By making their own plans and ignoring God's promise, plans, and purpose, Sarah and Abraham produced a counterfeit. This is always the consequence of impatient actions. We must learn patience—wait upon the Lord. If God has promised, God will fulfill. All must be done His way, His methods.

Fourth, Impatience gives birth to problems. Counterfeits always generate problems. When Hagar became pregnant by Abraham, Sarah became instantly jealous and Hagar had to run for her life (Genesis 16:6). Abraham found himself caught between two feuding women—not an enviable place for a man to be.

That which seemed so right to Abraham and Sarah gave Satan the handle he needed. The consequences are still with us. The Arabs are the descendants of Ishmael and the Israelites are the descendants of the true son of God's promise, Isaac. The battle between Ishmael and Isaac is still raging today. There is no doubt that all the Middle East problems of today are traceable back to these two half-brothers. When we take matters into our own hands and act in impatience, the ramifications of those acts may last for generations, as they have in the case of Abraham and Sarah.

We must learn how to wait if we are going to be contented and have peace—God's peace. Impatient actions can result in long lasting pain and suffering. We cannot run ahead of the Lord and expect success. When we become impatient with God, we become vulnerable to Satan's schemes and attacks. So how can we, in the right spirit and attitude, wait on the Lord?

We must understand that God waits with purpose.
Actually, God does not wait; rather, He does everything with perfect timing. We only perceive Him to be waiting or delaying. We may not understand, or ever know, why His plans unfold as they do and when they do, but here are some facts that will help us wait on the Lord.

1. God waits or delays for our growth. People usually grow by crises. Prosperity without pain is rarely spiritually productive. Most people do not become serious in prayer until they are faced with a difficult situation in their life. Paul wrote:

> *We exult (rejoice) in our tribulations, knowing that tribulation brings about perseverance; and perseverance, proven character; and proven character, hope.* (Romans 5:3-4).

And James also said:

> *Consider it all joy, my brethren, when you encounter various trials, knowing that the testing of our faith produces endurance, and let endurance have its perfect result, so that you may be perfect and complete, lacking nothing.* (James 1:2-3)

When God grows us, it often takes pressure, pain and time. But the pain has purpose and we can wait patiently when we rest in that Biblical fact. Note David's sorrow, pain, and frustration when he felt abandoned by the Lord:

> *How long, O Lord? Will You forget me forever? How long will You hide Your face from Me? How long shall I take counsel in my soul, having sorrow in my heart all the day? How long will my enemy be exalted over me? Consider and answer me, O Lord my God; Enlighten my eyes, or I will sleep the sleep of death, and my enemy will say, "I have overcome him," and my adversaries will rejoice when I am shaken. But I have trusted in Your lovingkindness; My heart shall rejoice in Your salvation. I will sing to the Lord, because He has dealt bountifully with me.* (Psalm 13)

David was struggling to understand why God had not come and rescued him, yet David did not lose his faith in the Lord. He looked forward and declared that he would end up singing to the Lord. This is the attitude and spirit you and I should have when we think the Lord is delaying His blessings. Remember, God often grows His children spiritually through what seems to us to be delayed deliverances.

2. God waits or delays in order to be glorified. He often waits until His promise, plan, and purpose are totally outside the ability of men. When He does act everyone knows who did it and that there is a sovereign God on the throne.

Abraham and Sarah are classic examples of this truth. Abraham evidently needed to learn firsthand that God will be glorified in all His promises. He promised them a child when they were far beyond child bearing years. Neither Abraham nor Sarah truly believed God when He said that Sarah would have a child. Fulfillment of God's promise was beyond the ability of man to produce.

The Lord did the same thing with Zacharias and Elizabeth. When they were young they prayed for a child. God delayed answering their prayer until they were older and when the time was right for John the Baptist to enter God's history: then He fulfilled His promise (Luke 1). It is likely that they had long ago ceased praying for a son, but the Lord did not forget.

3. God waits because He works in the circumstances of our lives. He works His plan and purpose through our lives, our politics, our economy, our culture, etc. He works His will on our turf—down here in our everyday activities; that takes time because we do not change easily or quickly. We learn best in our own environment. When He worked through all the Old Testament prophets and messengers, He did so in their own circumstances. He knows what it takes to bring each of us to the place where He has purposed us to be, so He creates the conditions then works in them to grow us and bring glory to Himself. Charles Spurgeon said, *"God is very good to those who trust in Him, and often surprises them with unlooked for blessings."*

We must wait with intelligent patience.
Patience is more than gritting our teeth and resolving to take whatever the Lord sends until He blesses. Patience needs something to hold on to, much like a lantern in the dark. Let me suggest three.

1. God's Word is a light in dark places. "Your word is a lamp to my feet and a light to my path" (Psalm 119:105). God's Word speaks to every crisis in life. His book is filled with promises of love, protection, grace, wisdom, security, forgiveness, guidance, assurance, comfort, and is our supply for every need. When we fully trust the Lord, we can hold fast to these promises until the storms and darkness pass. We do not cast the lantern of His light aside just because we may not like what we see.

2. God's person and presence is the second light in dark places. "*For You light my lamp; The LORD my God illumines my darkness*" (Psalm 18:28). When you are in crisis, focus on some unfailing attribute of God that fits your problem or crisis: power, love, grace, justice, wisdom, goodness, mercy, truth, eternity, omnipresence, etc. Hold fast to Him, to *Who He is*. Be Patient. If you see no light, then perhaps you should just be still and focus on Who He is; God sees everything clearly.

> *If I say, "Surely the darkness will overwhelm me, and the light around me will be night", Even the darkness is not dark to You, And the night is as bright as the day. Darkness and light are alike to You.* (Psalm 139:11-12)

The Word of God and the person and presence of God are solid and unfailing lanterns to hang onto through any crisis of life. The more we learn about our Lord, the more lanterns we will see.

3. God's Principles are the third lantern that shines in the dark times. How should we act while we patiently wait for the Lord to deliver us or provide guidance? We certainly should not be angry, revengeful, complaining, murmuring, or bitter. We should wait with patient love, faith, assurance, and expectation. Never race ahead of God.

> In some sense, the path to heaven is very safe—but in other respects, there is no road so dangerous! It is beset with difficulties. One wrong step—and down we go! And how easy it is to take that treacherous step—if grace is absent! [1]

A caution needs to be sounded here. We should never make Patience a cause for laziness. Certainly God wants us to be patient and wait on Him, but that does not mean that we merely close up shop on doing the things we are commanded to do in Scripture. Obedience often brings the fulfillment of promises. Sluggishness is deadly in DarkLand.

It is tough to wait patiently for the Lord to act. This is especially true if we are in pain and suffering. Even in the most trying or confusing circumstance, if we can rest in the fact that every situation God either causes or allows to come into our lives is working toward His purpose, for His glory, and for our good, He will give strength to patiently wait. The soldier must only move on the command of the Captain. Waiting honors the One who promised.

> Patience strengthens the spirit,
> Sweetens the temper,
> Stifles anger,
> Extinguishes envy,
> Subdues pride,
> Bridles the tongue,
> Restrains the hand,
> And tramples upon temptations. [2]

---

1   Charles Spurgeon, gracegems.org/b/spurgeongems.htm
2   George Horne (1730-1792), *The New Dictionary of Thoughts*, Standard Book Co., 1957, p. 470 (originally compiled in 1891 by Tyron Edwards, D.D.)

10

RECOGNITION

*Therefore encourage one another and build one another up,
just as you are doing.*
(1 Thessalonians 5:11, ESV)

Let no true-hearted man think that he is overlooked;
the King Himself has His eye upon him. [1]

One of the most needed and most neglected ministries is the ministry of recognition.

As fallen, sinful human beings, we have many common experiences which lead to difficulties for ourselves and others. Because of these experiences there is created within each of us a tendency to be somewhat insecure and needing reinforcement and recognition. The need for recognition is universal—no one is exempt. Every person wants recognition, which gives a sense of worth or significance, and every person needs a sense of worth and value for emotional health, encouragement, confidence, satisfaction, and a sense of accomplishment.

There is a Greek word which was used by some of the early philosophers which depicts this desire. Plato used it in describing his concept of the soul of man. He said the soul is three parts: *reason, epithymia* (desire), *and thymos* (the hunger for recognition). He argued that *thymos* is what motivates both the good and the bad actions of men. If uncontrolled, it drives men to war, to be cruel, and even to murder; yet the desire for recognition can also stimulate men to do good things. Regarding the good and noble actions, the core issue is motive—what is the motive? Regardless of what men are driven to do by *thymos,* everyone has this hunger.

Every child cries out for recognition. Haven't you watched as a child learned to ride a bike, draw a picture, or put together a puzzle? What do they do immediately? They look around to see who will notice them. "Look, Mommy!" or "Watch me, Daddy!" These are cries for encouraging recognition.

Grownups do the same thing, but we've learned to be somewhat less obvious about it. Just look around at the things which offer quick versions of recognition: sports, automobiles, clothes, electronic gadgets, homes, performances, positions, power, possessions. I wonder how often the cry "Hey, everybody look at me!" is underneath it all. "Look at my car, my clothes, or my position in life. See me! Notice me! Respect me!" There is no graduation from this need for significance as long as we are on this earth, no matter how old or how young. *Where* we look for it is key.

We have many very basic needs such as food, clothing, housing, personal security, and safety. In most cases, we can meet these needs in our own strength and abilities, but recognition and significance are beyond our ability to fulfill. Being dependent upon others, we are not in control of essentially fulfilling that need for significance. Thus, this longing within the human heart only adds to, and deepens, the complexity of the pursuit of satisfaction and significance. *To whom* we look for it is key.

Too often the drive for recognition leads to wrong pursuits, even dishonest activities, in order to gain fame, position, fortune, and power—all in order to obtain the desired recognition. Some people are boisterous, loud, critical, sarcastic, or constantly making cutting remarks; all are sinful symptoms of unsatisfied cravings for recognition sought from the wrong source.

Some folks can become very annoying in their attempts at being noticed. I remember a gentleman who represented his church at an assembly made up of folks from different churches. Issues were discussed and decisions made, but he could never find anything with which he agreed. He was always questioning, disagreeing, trying to dominate discussions on every issue. He was seeking attention and recognition, and became very annoying to everyone around him.

Interestingly, when the need for recognition is met, there is often a deep emotional response. No doubt you've seen it on different occasions when someone is being recognized for a good job they've done—sometimes tears and certainly huge smiles. Those tears speak volumes. A deep need has been met in that person's life and they are thankful for it. I bet you have experienced a long-awaited need to be met in your life and when it came it produced tears of gratitude.

When the need for recognition is met, it produces a higher standard for workers as well as in life itself. Many times I've heard employees of business corporations make the remark, "They (the corporate officers) don't appreciate the work we do." Where this attitude is present, the ability of employees to do their best is dampened. In fact, it breeds disloyalty to that company and reduces productivity both in substance and quality of work. Conversely, when the employees are recognized for jobs well done, the quality and quantity of productivity rise; a need is being met. This principle applies to all areas of our lives: marriage, family, children, work, play, church.

The good news is that our Omniscient Lord not only knows our need for recognition (He made us that way), but He gives recognition and significance to His children. Scripture records some specific cases for us. Scripture says that Moses was the meekest man on earth; Job was righteous; David was a man after God's own heart. That's pretty significant recognition in my book! And in our discouragements and toils, these names stand as signposts along the way to light the path and lift our spirits.

God provides recognition and gives significance to the lives of His Children. The Holy Spirit bestows spiritual gifts to those who are Christ's. Christians who humbly and without boasting exercise their Spiritual gift (or gifts) will certainly receive due recognition. I believe the Lord wants His people to stand out in this world. I do not believe that He intends His children to live a life of mediocrity; you can do that all by yourself. We are to stand out from the world, living above the average in speech, conduct, dress, desires, and affections. Let me say that again: *we are to stand out from the world, living above the average in speech, conduct, dress, desires, and affections.*

The first nine chapters of First Chronicles are comprised of genealogies—over 600 names are listed. In the middle of those 600 names is a man named *Jabez* whom the Lord gives special recognition. Perhaps you have never heard of Jabez, but the Lord intended that you know him because He has preserved his name for thousands of years. There are only two verses in the entire Bible that speak of this man, yet he is honored above hundreds of other people (1 Chronicles 4:9-10). The text begins *"Jabez was more honorable than his brothers..."* That's recognition! It is not my intent in this chapter to deal with all the arguments over Jabez's prayer, but simply to point out that he was recognized by God above nearly 600 other people and to point out why he was recognized.

Why did God honor Jabez? What was there about this man that was above average? What made him stand out? There are three things which I think made his life above average and can make your life above average as well as supply the right kind of recognition you need in your life as a Christian.

Jabez had great ambitions.
While Jabez's friends were content with being average or mediocre, he said, "I want God to bless me; I want something big; I want to do something significant with my life." Jabez didn't want to be ordinary. He wanted to grow and expand. *"Now Jabez called on the God of Israel, saying, 'Oh that You would bless me indeed and enlarge my border, and that Your hand might be with me, and that You would keep me from harm, that it may not pain me!'"* Great ambitions! He wanted great blessings from God and the protection from the Lord that he would not hurt anyone in obtaining this goal. Great attitude!

Most people in our churches have never really set goals or made plans for their lives. This is especially true with the younger generation. Several years ago while in the country of Ukraine I spent one Sunday night with a group of about 35 high school and college students. I asked them what their goals were for their lives—what they planned to accomplish and what occupation they planned to engage in? Only two out of the 35 students had any idea what they wanted to do after their graduation from high school or college. And they really didn't care about life goals beyond what they were doing at the moment. I doubt that the record would be much different with the young people in America. Sadly, this directionless drifting often continues through the years.

Most people are somewhat fatalistic about planning for life. They say, "Well, if God is going to bless me He will bless me." So the first principle for real and "right" recognition—living above average—is that you need a great and "right" ambition, ambition that does not conflict with the will of God, but goes in the same direction as His will. Be in communion with the Lord to ascertain what His will might be for your life; soak your mind in the Scriptures; ASK, SEEK, KNOCK; when He gives you directions and His peace in it, set goals to obtain it. If He is leading you to become a minister of the Gospel, prepare yourself—a good education in the field of theology, ministry, etc. The same is true in all the other disciplines of life— teaching, science, engineering, homemaking, child rearing, etc. It has been said that we need to dream about accomplishing our goals. If you don't have a dream, you are drifting. When you stop dreaming, you start dying. Our lives are not photo snapshots, they are motion pictures. Seek His direction and discernment for the right path and open doors.

The Lord has a purpose for your life, and your key to significance and recognition is in that purpose. Make His Purpose your purpose and your goal; make plans to reach that goal. Remember that whatever God's purpose for your life is, it's not average.

> The Lord can still use feeble instruments.
> Why not me?
>
> He may use persons who are not commonly called
> to great public engagements.
> Why not you? [2]

There are some major misconceptions that keep believers from having great ambitions and pursuing the best goals.

Fear is often confused with humility. Ever heard this said, "Oh, I could never achieve that." Could it be that the heart is just disguising an unwillingness to try while wearing a "Humble Badge"? The fear of failure is often branded as humbleness. When left to ourselves it's true that we can do nothing well, but the word of God comes alongside and speaks truth, "You cannot do it alone, but by God's grace you can do all." Set in the context of hard times, Paul wrote, *"I can do all things through Him who strengthens me"* (Philippians 4:13). Fear of failure must never be disguised under a cloak of humility. Great ambitions are born out of faith and confidence in the Lord, *not fear*.

Laziness is not to be confused with contentment. It is true that Paul said, *"I have learned to be content in whatever circumstance I am"* (Philippians 4:11); Paul did *not* say, "I have learned not to strive for goals, ambitions, or any future desires." Even though some of his desires might not be reached yet, Paul learned to enjoy to the fullest what he had in the present. He certainly did not mean that he ceased striving and reaching to attain his objective. He did not abandon his ambitions; what was his major ambition? Here it is, *"that I may know Him and the power of His resurrection and the fellowship of His sufferings, being conformed to His death"* (Philippians 3:10; see also Philippians 3:7-11).

Suppose your fourth grader said, "Mom, Dad, I've learned to be content with the amount of education I have; I think I'll quit school!" I suspect that the ambitions of that child might change rapidly. Don't confuse laziness with contentment. Are you content to have Bibles lying around the house, but you're too lazy to open, read, and study? There's no place for laziness in the things of God. *"The sluggard buries his hand in the dish; He is weary of bringing it to his mouth again"* (Proverbs 26:15). It is pretty telling when one is too lazy to eat—both physically or spiritually.

Small Thinking is not to be mistaken as Spirituality. This is a relative of *fear*. Have you ever heard someone say, "Well, I serve the Lord in my own little way?" That is small thinking. "Well, you know, I can't do anything that makes a difference." "This is the way God made me, and I'm too old to change now." Small Thinking! Is the power of God limited? Scripture doesn't label such statements and motives as commendable.

Don't confuse fear with humility, laziness with contentment, or spirituality with small thinking. It all has to do with obedience to the Lord as He instructs us in His Word. Soak your mind in the Word of God, then do what He says. His grace is sufficient for whatever He puts before you. Then you will have righteous and great ambitions; then you will be recognized in His time.

Jabez had a growing faith.
Not only did he have *great ambitions,* but he also had *a growing faith.* His faith was great enough that he expected answers to his prayers. The great missionary, William Carey, was like Jabez when he said, "Attempt great things for God; expect great things from God."

There are some interesting things about Jabez. Yes, he was *"more honorable than his brothers"* and yet there is no mention of *talents, wealth,* or *education.* He obviously was a common man but he had an uncommon faith.

Jabez's faith was simple, *"Oh that You would bless me indeed and enlarge my border, and that Your hand might be with me, and that You would keep me from harm that it may not pain me!"* His prayer was not contrary to God's will because God answered his prayer. *"And God granted him what he requested."* Jabez believed that his ambitions were not contrary to God's will so he asked big; God granted big.

Not only does Jabez appear to be a common man without talent, education, or wealth, but the name "Jabez" means "painful." In birth he caused his mother so much pain and grief that she named him "Painful."

Some believe that Jabez was either handicapped in some way or he was an unwanted and unloved child. Either would bring pain. How would you like to go through life wearing the name "Painful" and knowing that you were evidently the source of pain to someone? Notwithstanding, his faith was stronger than his handicap. Note one of his great ambitions: he prayed *"let Your hand be with me, and keep me from harm, so that I will not cause any pain."* (1 Chronicles 4:10, CSB). Had he caused so much pain to his mother that he did not want to cause pain to anyone else? That seems to be part of his great desire and request. That is a sign of godly humility.

What is your handicap or baggage? Is it physical? Is it spiritual? Is it an unhappy childhood? Is it frustrating or painful circumstances? Don't live in DarkLand just because you think all is darkness *everywhere*. Believe God. Don't cling to baggage that Christ says to cast away or lay on Him. Why not start living above these handicaps, think scripturally, have great ambitions, grow in commitment to Christ. Did not our Lord say, *"all things are possible to him who believes"* (Mark 9:23)? Jabez had great ambitions and a growing faith.

He had a genuine prayer life.
With simple dedication and the prayer life of a common man, Jabez obtained for himself honor from the Lord. He is still being honored and recognized every time this passage in First Chronicles 4 is read.

Why hesitate to ask the Lord for what is on your heart? Perhaps you fear that your requests are selfish, so you hesitate. Perhaps you're not confident that you're praying in the will of God. There are three things about Jabez's prayer that will help us in our prayer life. Consider each and ponder your own desires.

First, Jabez desired God's Power in his life. He desired a power greater than what he found within himself; he prayed, *"Oh that you would bless me..."* In other words, "I want Your power in my life." Then he becomes specific, *"enlarge my border...and keep me from evil."* At first it may appear that his prayer was selfish, but evidently it wasn't, because God answered it. *"God granted him what he requested"* (1 Chronicles 4:10).

Ambitions are a necessary motivator in our lives. Some ambitions are good and some are bad, but everyone has ambitions of some sort. That which determines whether your ambitions are good or bad is not their greatness or smallness, but the motive; "motive" is determined by God's analysis and scale.

God recognized this common man and his uncommon requests. The message of Jabez throughout history is that prayers are not answered according to the magnitude of the request, but on what we want to accomplish and the motive of the heart. For our motives to be right we must have the power of God in our lives; Jabez prayed for God's power in his life.

Second, he prayed for God's presence in his life. He prayed *"that your hand be with me."* Here again we see the same thought: if we do not have the *power* and *presence* of God in our lives we cannot pray in the will of the Lord. Our motives will be wrong and unacceptable before the Lord. If our heart and mind are not filled with the Holy Spirit of God, our motives, desires, and prayers will rise from the throne of *self.*

Further, the more blessings and "territory" that the Lord grants will also bring more responsibility, more demands, more pressures, and a need for a more conscious presence of the Lord in our lives. So Jabez prayed for the presence of the Lord in His life.

Third, Jabez prayed for God's protection on his life. The more God blesses us, the more protection we need from Sin, Self, Satan, and the influences and snares of the world. Jabez seems to have been keenly aware of this truth, so he prayed for the protection of the

Lord on his life. If God blesses you with possessions, you will be attacked by the world from without and tempted from within. In the days of Jabez, one's influence grew with the land one owned. He was well aware of this and the dangers and responsibilities involved. He knew his own weaknesses and he asked for protection.

As an old wise Christian man was going out of his church one Sunday morning, he met an acquaintance whom he had not seen for several years. In their brief discussion he said to his old acquaintance, "I understand you are in great danger." It was said in all seriousness, and was heard with surprise. The friend addressed was not aware of any danger and eagerly inquired what was meant. The wise old Christian replied, "I have been informed that you are getting rich."

It's been said that there are four classes of people when it comes to the matter of wealth in money or possessions. (1) There are those who are rich in this world's possessions but poor toward the Lord. (2) There are those who are poor in this world but rich toward the Lord. (3) There are those who are poor in both this world and the next. (4) Some are rich in the world's possessions, and because they have a righteous attitude toward possessions, they are rich toward the Lord also. Those in this last category are few; not many are able to be rich in material possessions without being attached to or consumed by those possessions. Perhaps Jabez fully understood this and prayed for the Lord's protection.

How often have you known a common man reared in an ordinary home who attained wealth and his whole life changed, but not for the better? Those who once knew him say, "This is not the man I knew growing up, why is he different?" The difference is that he is now possessed by his possessions. Yet there are other people who obtained wealth but did not change; they were not possessed by their possessions; they honored God and gave Him their gratitude and worship. These are the few who were protected by God's grace from being addicted and devoted to their wealth. Wealth and the power that often attends it are mighty seducers and DarkLand is full of people looking for recognition in them. Jabez wanted God's protection from powers too great for him to face. Paul wrote *"the love of money is the root of all sorts of evil..."* (1 Timothy 6:10). Notice he did not say that **money** was the root of all kinds of evil, but the *"love of money."*

A faithful old preacher of the gospel was visited by a man who was an obvious lover of money. The preacher had made a statement in his Sunday sermon which disturbed the wealthy man greatly and he came to the preacher with questions. The wise and aged man of God evaluated the man's attitude toward money quite well. He reached into his pocket, took out a coin, and opened his worn Bible to a place where the word "God" was recorded. He asked the man, "Can you see that word 'God'?" "Of course!" the man replied. The aged servant of the Lord then placed the coin over the word "God" and asked the man, "Can you see it now?" The man quickly understood the message and was led to commit himself to the Lord Jesus Christ. The gleam and glitter of money often blinds the sinner to the glory of God in the face of Jesus Christ.

There is a path into DarkLand paved with gold, and the glitter of it blinds those who take it and remain on it. At its end is a graveyard, and those blinded by gold and greed never see that they are walking in the midst of death.

True wealth is found in knowing Christ, His great salvation, and the real and eternal riches which He bestows on all who trust and obey Him. This world and all that it offers cannot satisfy the hearts of men.

Don't miss the sequence of Jabez's prayer. He asked for *greater possessions,* then he prayed for *God's power, presence,* and *protection.* His heart was right, his prayer was answered and his recognition was on time. He demonstrates to us a great ambition, a growing faith, and a genuine prayer life *"God granted him what he requested." "He was more honorable than his brothers."*

Yet we have more than did Jabez in his day. For God to have your name written on the palms of His hands is the greatest recognition. He wears you upon His heart. You are His sheep and He knows you by name. The hairs of your head are numbered and He knows your thoughts and yearnings. All has been done. A place is prepared. A banquet spread. He will wipe your tears away. Does every Christian not desire to hear the words of His Savior, "Well done, thou good and faithful servant"?

That's Recognition!

---

1 Charles Spurgeon, *Faith's Checkbook*, Christian Art Gifts, 2009, July 9 devotion
2 Charles Spurgeon, *Faith's Checkbook*, Christian Art Gifts, 2009, June 21 devotion

11

PERSECUTION

His sheep feed in the midst of wolves—yet are safely preserved;
for, though they cannot see Him—His eye and
His heart are ever upon them! [1]

Persecution for Christ's sake is not an issue often talked about in America. Perhaps most Americans who say they are Christians are not living in such a Christ-like manner that the world hates them enough to persecute them. However, in the last few years Christianity has begun to feel the sting of the world's hatred because of our moral stand regarding such things as abortion, euthanasia, stem cell research, same sex marriages, homosexuality, public expression of our faith, etc. Actually, the world hates us for just about any reason they can find. Think about the hatred and vitriol expressed when Christmas-time comes. Just the sound of a Christmas carol or the sight of a Nativity scene stirs the world's rage. Christ told us to expect this; the world hated Him when He lived among men and the world will hate His people. Expect it!

The question is: "How should we respond when people cause us grief, troubles, pain, and discomfort on account of our love for Christ and determination to follow and obey Him?" Joseph of the Old Testament is a classic example of pain, sorrows, and troubles brought on by others because of a godly character.

Joseph was the second youngest of twelve brothers, and the favorite of his father. Can you imagine the jealousy between those boys and Joseph? That jealousy was so deep and bitter that his brothers threw

Joseph into a pit, intending to leave him to die there. But God had other plans and sent a nomadic band of Ishmaelite merchants by their campsite. The brothers sold Joseph to the passing merchants instead of killing him; the merchants took him to Egypt. *"So they pulled him up and lifted Joseph out of the pit and sold him to the Ishmaelites for twenty shekels of silver. Thus they brought Joseph into Egypt"* (Genesis 37:28).

In a foreign country, Joseph didn't know anyone; he couldn't speak the language; he didn't know the customs of the culture; he found himself a slave. On top of all that, his master's wife attempted to seduce him. Joseph refused her seductive efforts and, in doing so, enraged her. Filled with fury and seeking revenge she falsely accused Joseph of rape. Although innocent, Joseph was cast into a dark prison dungeon. He was lonely, disappointed in his brothers and his Egyptian master, homesick and hurting.

Here was a young man persecuted beyond anything we could imagine, that not only from a godless world, but also by his own family. But those circumstances, although cruel and vicious, did not change Joseph's character except for the good.

> The problem of life, is to keep the heart warm and kindly—amid all injustice and wrong; to keep the spirit brave and cheerfully—in the midst of all that is hard in life's circumstances and conditions; to be true, and right, and strong—in all moral purpose and deed, however others may act toward us.
>
> Our inner life should not be affected by external experiences. Right is right, no matter what others around us may do. We must be true—no matter if all the world is false—even false to us. We must be unselfish and loving—though even our nearest friends prove selfish and cruel to us. We must keep our spirit

strong, cheerful and hopeful—though adversities and misfortunes seem to leave us nothing of the fruit of all our labors. [2]

But God was with Joseph; he will be forever honored in Holy Scripture. Joseph was a picture and foreshadowing of Christ Jesus. His years of hardship and suffering were the dark canvas on which God displayed power and glory and redemption. However, as a consequence of his honesty and character, the workings of God's Providence elevated Joseph to a position of power second only to the Pharaoh, king of Egypt.

Many years later, God's Providence brought Joseph's brothers to Egypt, then to Joseph for help. They traveled from their home all the way to Egypt, unknowingly fulfilling the purpose of God. Years had passed. Never dreaming that their younger brother was even alive, much less in such a high position of power, the brothers did not recognize him, but Joseph knew them.

Scripture leaves no guesswork as to the heart and character of Joseph. When he finally reveals himself to his brothers, he seeks to dispel their fears and guilt. Joseph spoke to his brothers: *"Now do not be grieved or angry with yourselves, because you sold me here, for God sent me before you to preserve life. For the famine has been in the land these two years, and there are still five years in which there will be neither plowing nor harvesting. God sent me before you to preserve for you a remnant in the earth, and to keep you alive by a great deliverance. Now, therefore, it was not you who sent me here, but God; and He has made me a father to Pharaoh and lord of all his household and ruler over all the land of Egypt"* (Genesis 45:5-8). In other words, "God used your evil to bring about His purpose for your good."

Because of the life and attitude of Joseph as he endured persecution, we can gain wisdom. Joseph seems to have recognized three important truths that enabled him to hang in there. In these three things we too can find strengthening encouragement when we suffer persecution.

Lessons from Joseph
First, we can be assured that *God knows and sees everything we go through and He cares.* Joseph was convinced that God knew every pain he had and that He cared. There is a phrase which is repeated five times through this whole episode of Joseph's life, namely, *"But the Lord was with Joseph."* That phrase appears at every major event in His life. Even Pharaoh recognized that the Lord was with Joseph. Pharaoh did not know Joseph's God, but he knew that some divine power was with Joseph in a very mighty way. Note the words of Pharaoh: *"Then Pharaoh said to his servants, 'Can we find a man like this, in whom is a divine spirit'? So Pharaoh said to Joseph, 'Since God has informed you of all this, there is no one so discerning and wise as you are'"* (Genesis 41:38-39).

Even in his days and nights of greatest pain, and when it seemed that all things were unjust and wrong, Joseph knew the Lord was with him. In the dark events which were thrust upon him, Joseph found the strength and encouragement to live the life that eventually brought him to be trusted by the Pharaoh of Egypt. Endurance in faithfulness to the Lord will bring ultimate reward; perhaps not in this life, but certainly in the next, but glory to Him in both. "We judge things by their present appearances, but the Lord sees them in their consequences." [3]

If you really believe that there is no time or circumstance in your life when He is not with you, will you collapse under persecution or suffering? God held Joseph in His hand even though outward appearances disguised it. He holds you too. When we trust that God is with us, we then walk by faith not by sight. Clouds of darkness do not change the reality and unchangeableness of the Lord's purpose and presence.

> Doubt sees the obstacles,
> Faith sees the way!
> Doubt sees the darkest night,
> Faith sees the day!
> Doubt dreads to take a step,
> Faith soars on high!
> Doubt questions, "Who believes?"
> Faith answers, "I!"
> (Author Unknown)

The second truth is *Joseph knew that he was responsible for his reaction to persecution*. Joseph could have argued the sovereignty of God as an excuse to give in to temptations and blame God for his circumstances and persecution, but he acted rightly and responsibly on every occasion. Joseph didn't blame God when his brothers threw him into a pit to die. We don't read of him accusing God of planting the evil in the hearts of his brothers or causing them to sell him into slavery. He did not blame God for the situation when Potiphar's wife tried to seduce him. He did not blame God when he was thrown into prison. Joseph obviously believed that God was sovereign in all things; he also recognized his own duty and responsibility to his God.

The sovereignty of God is never to be used as a crutch or excuse for wrong actions and attitudes. Unquestionably, God is sovereign and nothing takes place without either His direct decree or His permission. But even though His decrees and His permissive will together ultimately accomplish His eternal purpose, they can never be used as an excuse for sin. To deny our responsibilities is to charge God with being the author of our sins.

We are living in a "blame game society"—every "bad" thing that happens to us or every sin we commit is the fault of someone else. This game is not new; it started in the Garden of Eden. Adam blamed God for his sin by implying that if God had not given him the woman (Eve) he wouldn't have sinned (Genesis 3:12). It was all her fault—and God's fault. This is a cowardly hideous tendency of fallen, sinful men, to blame others for their sins. I suspect that you've played this game as well. However, the Bible doesn't consent to our playing the "Not My Fault" game. We will stand before God personally and be held fully responsible for our actions. No excuses will be accepted on the Day of Judgment. Joseph never blamed; Joseph never became bitter; Joseph trusted.

The third truth in Joseph's story is *God's purpose will be accomplished.* Joseph related this to his brothers when he said, *"As for you, you meant evil against me, but God meant it for good in order to bring about this present result, to preserve many people alive"* (Genesis 50:20). Long before it was written in Scripture by the Apostle Paul, it was written on Joseph's heart: *"We know that God causes all things to work together for good to those who love God, to those who are called according to His purpose"* (Romans 8:28). This does not necessarily mean that all things are working to bring about our temporal ease, or comfort, or happiness in this world, but it does mean that the ultimate goal God has for us is to make us like His Son, the Lord Jesus Christ (Romans 8:29).

The only explanation to the story of Joseph is that God is sovereign and works all things according to the counsel of His own will (Ephesians 1:11). Joseph was nearly killed, sold into slavery, accused of rape, put into prison. The long treacherous road winding through dark events brought Joseph to the position of God's Purpose as the most powerful man in Egypt, except for the Pharaoh. And from that place of honor and authority he became the source of life to his own family and many others.

When we come to understand that God is working every event in the life of His children for their ultimate good, and that He always works in a way which brings glory to Himself, we are strengthened and encouraged in the most difficult circumstances of persecution and maltreatment. To the degree that we grasp and rest in this Scriptural fact, we glorify Him. There is no anchor for the storm or compass in the wilderness if we believe that God has no purpose in allowing us to be persecuted; Paul said, *"we know"* all these events are working for our ultimate good. All things serve God.

In a letter to his thirteen year old adopted niece, John Newton wrote,

> I wish for you my dear child, to think much of the Lord's governing providence. It extends to the minutest concerns. He rules and manages all things; but in so secret a way, that most people think that He does nothing. When, in reality—He does ALL!

So the lessons we learn from Joseph are these: God knows and sees everything we go through and He cares. We must, like Joseph, take responsibility for our actions in adverse circumstances; God's purpose will be accomplished. Knowing these things won't lessen the pain of persecutions, but it will give strength to endure in a manner which molds us and gives glory to Christ.

Coping with Persecution
You may be experiencing a harsh and thorny road in life; strained relationships may exist with your own family members who don't like your Christ-likeness and integrity. Someone may be angry with you concerning something about which you are completely innocent, yet you have become the target of hostility and bitterness. Such had been Joseph's situation and he served time in prison because of it.

The question I want us to answer now is how did Joseph deal with events in the dark places of his life? God teaches and refines us bit by bit as only He knows that we are able to bear it, and with no more pressure than is required for His intended outcome in us. We must come to know and truly believe not only in His great power and omniscience, but also see our own weakness and inabilities apart from Him.

First, Joseph did not give in to self-pity. When overtaken by a storm at sea, the wise mariner does not turn from the storm and stop all engines, but rather heads the ship straight into the face of the storm. In the face of darkness and storm, there's no wisdom in sitting down and having a crying pity party. When faced with a difficult situation, don't run from it; face it head on in the strength of the Lord and faith in His Providence.

Second, Joseph did not make hasty decisions in the dark; he waited. He was submissive and full of faith that the Lord would bring him through it all, trusting that the Lord had a purpose for all things.

> As to daily occurrences, it is best to trust that a daily portion of comforts and crosses—each one the most suitable to our case—is adjusted and appointed by the hand which was once nailed to the cross for us! We must trust that where the path of duty and prudence leads us—there is the best situation we could possibly be in, at that time. [4]

Third, Joseph did not charge God foolishly. He did not grit his teeth and accuse God of mismanaging his life by allowing such great difficulties. This is different from the attitude recommended by the "grin and bear it" crowd. Instead, Joseph patiently submitted to the will of God. Waiting is not the same as doing nothing.

Fourth, Joseph forgave his brothers. Forgiveness can be difficult depending upon the depth of the "cut" as well as our likeness to Christ. In Acts 7 we read of another young man whose heart revealed a character not unlike that of Joseph. When Stephen was being stoned he died asking the Lord to forgive those who were killing him. We are most like our Lord when we can forgive like that. Although the wrong to Stephen was great and the pain was unto death, his prayer reflected the character and glory of his Lord and Savior.

I once read a story about a young lady who was in college and during the summer months she sold books to help with her college expenses. One day while she was out working to sell books, she was attacked, raped, and murdered. The man was apprehended, tried, convicted, and sentenced to life in prison. The girl's godly parents came to the place where they forgave the man who killed their daughter and began going to the prison to witness to him about Christ. That, my friend, is beyond the ability of any human in their own strength. It was Christ-like.

Sources of Strength and Encouragement
By examining the life of Joseph you should see at least four sources of encouragement, strength, and light when you are experiencing some form of persecution or suffering because of someone else's sinfulness.

First, God's PLAN encourages and strengthens. Read again Genesis 50:20 and Romans 8:28. God has a purpose, and a plan to accomplish that purpose. God does not have problems, He only has plans. His purpose and plans are greater than any problem or circumstance in any of our lives. Remember, all things serve Him.

God's great purpose for his children is to make them like Christ; He has a plan for your life to accomplish that purpose. Each of His children is an individual; He knows exactly what is needed for you. There will be some dark valleys and you must learn to trust Him and walk by faith. Storms will come, but He won't sink your boat. When the storm passes, the Light shines brighter than ever, and you are more equipped for the next one.

For the Christ-follower, life is a series of calms and storms, light and darkness as we mature in the faith. The smile of God may be hidden from you if you are on His anvil, but it is in the dark that the sparks from each blow give evidence that God is hammering out the character that He wants to see in us.

It is not easy to rest in these truths when we are battered and beaten by persecution and Giant Despair. But later on when looking back we can sometimes see the good that God has brought about in our life as He guided us through and kept us from camping out in the Valley of Despondency. When we understand this we are prepared to look back and say to people who hurt us or persecuted us, "you meant it for bad, but God meant it for good; you meant it to destroy me, but God meant it to develop me; you meant it to tear me down, but God meant it to build me up; you meant it to weaken me, but God meant it to strengthen me." It's at that point we become thankful and can do what Paul admonishes us to do: *"Always giving thanks for all things..."* (Ephesians 5:20) because we know that our blessed Savior is working out His plan for our lives through all the difficulties.

> Jesus Himself was a "man of sorrow and acquainted with grief" for our sakes. He drank the whole cup of unmixed wrath for us! Shall we then refuse to taste of the cup of affliction at His appointment, especially when His wisdom and love prepare it for us—and He proportions every circumstance to our strength; when He puts it into our hands, not in anger—but in tender

mercy—to do us good, to bring us near to Himself, and when He sweetens every bitter sip with those comforts which none but He can give? [5]

Second, God's PROMISES encourage and strengthen. It is said that there are over 7,000 promises in God's word for believers to anchor their faith in. They are like signed blank checks. They are there with the Savior's signature on them, "In the name of Jesus." Let me remind you of only a few of these promises to which we can go when we are being mistreated or persecuted.

> *Many are the afflictions of the righteous,*
> *but the Lord delivers him out of them all.*
> (Psalm 34:19)

> *Cast your burden upon the Lord and He will sustain you;*
> *He will never allow the righteous to be shaken.*
> (Psalm 55:22)

> *Do not fear, for I am with you;*
> *Do not anxiously look about you, for I am your God.*
> *I will strengthen you, surely I will help you,*
> *surely I will uphold you with My righteous right hand.*
> (Isaiah 41:10)

> *Consider it all joy, my brethren, when you encounter various trials, knowing that the testing of your faith produces endurance, and let endurance have its perfect result, so that you may be perfect and complete, lacking nothing.* (James 1:2-4)

Surely you can find and apply some of these promises to your circumstance and commit them to memory. One man put scripture verses on his car's sun visor, and every time he stopped at a traffic light he would read one. He memorized hundreds of passages by simply utilizing the time while stopped in traffic. Memorizing promises of God is a healthy practice. Having the promises of our Savior in our memory bank will be of great comfort when we are going through rough terrain in life.

Paul reminds us that all scriptures, not just the promises, are beneficial to us for encouragement and instruction when he wrote to the church at Rome:

> *For whatever was written in early times was written for our instruction, so that through perseverance and the encouragement of the Scripture we might have hope.* (Romans 15:4)

The record of Joseph was written to encourage, and instruct us today as well as people of long ago.

> *You do well to pay attention as to a lamp shining in a dark place, until the day dawns and the morning star arises in your hearts.* (1 Peter 1:19).

Third, God's PEOPLE encourage and strengthen. True Christians are caring people who know in their heart and mind both the responsibility and privilege to pray for one another, help one another, encourage one another, and admonish one another. The people of God are a body of blood-washed sinners united in their Savior and King the Lord Jesus Christ.

In both Romans 12 and First Corinthians 12, Paul pictures the church using the metaphor of a physical body. In both passages he illustrates how each member of the body is dependent on all other members of the body and how they work together in unity. He emphasizes this unity by stating, *"Rejoice with those who rejoice, and weep with those who weep"* (Romans 12:15). *"If one member suffers, all the members suffer with it; if one member is honored, all the members rejoice with it"* (1 Corinthians 12:26). We are so united in Christ that we actually enter into the experiences of the other members of the body of Christ—if one hurts they all hurt, and if one is rejoicing, they all rejoice with him. This is the recipe for encouragement to meet the most difficult circumstances of life.

The Lord intends for His church to be a support system, but we can't be a support system if we don't know each other. This is why Bible study, Sunday school, and worshiping together are so vital to the spiritual health of believers. These are your support groups when the storms of life surge over you and the light of His face seems obscured. These are the people who will be there to pray with you and encourage you.

Our loving Lord allows us to get in situations where we are tried and tested, then He comforts us through his people, the church. Take careful note of this promise;

> *Blessed be the God and Father of our Lord Jesus Christ, the Father of mercies and God of all comfort, who comforts us in all our affliction so that we will be able to comfort those who are in any affliction with the comfort with which we ourselves are comforted by God.* (2 Corinthians 1:3-4)

This means that every difficult experience God allows you to go through is preparing you to be a comfort to others who may have to pass through the same dark maze that you have. The greatest comfort I received when my daughter was killed came from people who had gone through similar circumstances. In God's Providence, they had been prepared to comfort me as well as others who would go through the same Valley of Sorrow.

Fourth, God's PRESENCE encourages and strengthens. Because God is omnipotent (all-powerful), omniscient (all-knowing), and omnipresent (always everywhere present), we can surely take courage. There is never a time, place, or circumstance when God is not present with His children. When Jesus sent out His disciples, He made them a promise and that promise applies to you and me as well. *"I am with you always, even to the end of the age"* (Matthew 28:20). In another place He promises: *"I will never desert you, nor will I ever forsake you"* (Hebrews 13:5). In days and nights of trouble and persecution He is at our side. Our minds may be clouded with sorrow and confused; our frame may be feeble; our knees may be weak; yet His arm of power supports us. There is no dark to Him; He has already walked every path.

I am convinced that if we could grab hold of the truth that the Lord is always present with us, just as He was with the three Hebrew boys in the fiery furnace and with Joseph in the pit and prison, we would not fear any deluge of troubles He chooses to send our way.

A winding dirt road followed the river through the mountains of eastern Kentucky to the farm where I grew up. In the summertime there was a section of the way where the tree branches which arched over the road were thick with leaves and vines making the path dark even in the daytime. The narrow road was pitch-black at night—even the light of the moon couldn't shine through the dense overhead canopy. I still remember well the times that I had to walk home at night, alone; it was the longest mile ever. But when my dad was with me, I had no fear at all because he was with me to protect me, all the way home. Now, if my heavenly Father is always with me as I walk through life, why should I fear anything? He is with me to protect me from all harm and He will get me home safely. We are

Christ's sheep and we live with wolves all around. But, He is our Shepherd and responsible for preserving and defending the sheep and lambs; His eye and love are forever on them.

> He rules and manages all things but in so secret a way that most people think that He does nothing, when, in reality—He does ALL. [6]

Perhaps you have been hurt deeply by someone, as Joseph was. It might be a brother, a sister, a parent, a beloved child, or trusted friend who has wounded or betrayed you. Don't give in to anger, self-pity, resentment, or bitterness. Look to the *plan* of God, the *promises* of God, the *people* of God, and the *presence* of God—these are His gifts for you. He will never abandon you or fail you. In Him are provided the encouragement and strength which you need to walk through dark places of persecution.

> Which of God's children have not cause to say, "My soul is among lions!" But our Shepherd stops their mouths, or only permits them to gape and roar, and show their teeth. He does not allow them to bite and tear us at their will. Let us trust our Shepherd—and all shall be well. [7]

---

1 John Newton, *Cardiphonia*, Morgan and Scott LD, 1911, p. 366
2 J.R. Miller, gracegems.org/miller
3 John Newton, *Cardiphonia*, Morgan and Scott LD, 1911, p. 405
4 John Newton, *Cardiphonia*, Morgan and Scott LD, 1911, p. 367
5 John Newton, *The Works of John Newton, Volume 6*, Hamilton, Adams, and Co., 1820, reprinted by Banner of Truth Trust, 1988, pg. 8
6 John Newton, *The Works of John Newton, Volume 6*, Hamilton, Adams, and Co., 1820, reprinted by Banner of Truth Trust, 1988, pg. 309
7 John Newton, *The Works of John Newton, Volume 2*, Hamilton, Adams, and Co., 1820, reprinted by Banner of Truth Trust, 1988, pg. 177-178

12

FEAR

> Ye fearful saints, fresh courage take,
> The clouds you so much dread
> Are big with mercy, and shall break
> In blessings on your head. [1]

> Eternity to the godly is a day that has no sunset;
> eternity to the wicked is a night that has no sunrise. [2]

In the dark our minds can manufacture things to fear. Fear is one of the most powerful of all emotions; it often causes uncommon behavior: sometimes violent, sometimes heroic, sometimes cowardly. Fear causes some people to draw back from situations, restrains progress, dulls creativity, and often sets the stage for failure. It can be a tyrannical ruler of men's souls, a cruel taskmaster ready to lash us at the first sign of discouragement, doubt, disappointment, or failure.

The Bible speaks of fear holding people in bondage. Referring to mankind in Hebrews 2:15, the writer says: *"who through fear of death were all their lifetime subject to bondage."* Christ described the events surrounding His return: *"men's hearts will fail them from fear"* (Luke 21:26). Fear can paralyze; some folks are so afraid of dying they never have joy in living.

I read about a man who kept a Doberman Pincher in his place of business to stand guard at night. A man broke in one night. The Doberman kept him at bay in a corner barking, snapping, and showing his carnivore fangs as he snarled and stalked the man all night. Out of fear and terror, the man turned gray headed overnight. This probably is an exaggerated story, but it may demonstrate some fruits of fear.

Fears come in different forms. Young men's fears are usually associated with social acceptance, careers, promotions, money, and going to the dentist. Most women's fears are associated with marriage, being loved, growing old, gaining weight, living alone, and bugs, snakes, and spiders. The elderly have fears related to nursing homes, diseases, losing their mate, uncaring children, insurance, financial security, being ignored or forgotten, and sometimes death. Women express their fears with tears; men often try to just be macho.

What is fear? It's a normal human reaction to some perceived danger; fear always has an object. We all have fears of some sort. By creation God equipped us with this emotion as a means of survival. When we sense danger, fear automatically emerges and we react to the danger; the body and mind work together to fight or flee. Some fears are more in the category of anxiety or worry, coming to the forefront when we are faced with uncertainty or doubts.

We all have fears, and not all fears are bad. We ought to fear that which threatens injury, whether mentally or physically. Fearing that which is dangerous is a sign of spiritual maturity.

> *The prudent man sees evil and hides himself.*
> *The naïve proceed and pay the penalty.*
> (Proverbs 27:12)

We are commanded to fear God.

> *Fear God and keep His commandments*
> *for this is the whole duty of man.*
> (Ecclesiastes 12:13, ESV)

The fear of God is the beginning of wisdom.
(Proverbs 9:10)

The fear of God is not a "scaredy-cat" kind of fear. It is a "respect-fear," not unlike a son's fear of a loving father, a reverential fear, a fear born of knowing and drawing near to the burning holiness of God.

There are actually two kinds of fear. There is a *virtuous fear*, which is the effect of faith. This is the fear (respect, reverence, awe) for the Lord. Then there is a *vicious fear*, the offspring of doubt and unbelief keeping us in bondage to our anxieties and worries. One is the root of hope and the other the source of despair. The first will lead us away from DarkLand; the last will take you by the hand for a tour of its dead-end paths. The kind of fear we have, virtuous or vicious, will depend on our knowledge, estimations, thoughts, and opinions of the Lord Jesus Christ. If we truly know Christ, believe Him, and daily walk and commune with Him, there is little room for vicious fear to squeeze in and pitch a tent in our hearts. Isn't it comforting to know that the Captain of our soul knew that there would be times when His soldiers' hearts would be fearful? He gave us no less than 366 "fear nots" in our Bible. These "fear nots" cover every conceivable circumstance of life.

We need to gain biblical and experiential knowledge of how to conquer the *vicious fears* which creep into our lives. The Captain has provided armor for the battle: are you wearing it? Do you know Scripture? It's your weapon against fear! Search for one of those 366 "fear nots" which fit your circumstance. That's one way to react to *vicious* fear: holding fast to the words of Scripture and the power of the unchangeable God who stands behind every word. We fear what we can't control; our Father controls everything!

> *God is our refuge and strength, a very present help in trouble. Therefore we will not fear, though the earth should change and though the mountains slip into the heart of the sea; though its waters roar and foam, though the mountains quake at its swelling pride.* (Psalm 46:1-3)

Scriptural principles will guide through any fearful situation regardless of the circumstances whether in life or in facing death or eternity. These following principles from Psalm 46 are very simple, yet effective and within reach of every person who is a child of God.

The Protection of the Lord is Provided: "God is our refuge"
What an encouraging statement that is! The word translated "refuge" literally means "a place to which one can go quietly for protection." Under the Old Testament Law, when a person accidentally, without premeditation, and unintentionally broke a law that required death as punishment, there were *cities of refuge* (Numbers 35:6) to which the perceived lawbreaker could flee and have protection from the relatives of those whom he had accidentally injured or killed. God instituted cities of refuge to protect a person who was not a criminal.

In Psalm 46, the psalmist pictures *God* as the place of refuge and safety. There's only one place of refuge for any sinner, only one safe haven from God's just condemnation on sin, its awful consequences, and sentence of death. The Lord is our Refuge: in Him are forgiveness, joy, peace, and assurance. He is all we need, regardless of the form fear takes. Vicious fear is an emotion that can only give birth to cowardice. Vicious fear whispers to us that our greatest dread will overtake us, but God is our Refuge; He is our Shield.

> God spoke to Abram: *"After these things the word of the Lord came to Abram in a vision, saying, 'do not*

> *be afraid, Abram. I am your shield, your exceedingly great reward.'"* (Genesis 15:1, KJV, emphasis mine)

God is our Defender against the accuser. The Apostle Paul wrote to the church at Rome: *"Who shall bring a charge against God's elect? It is God who justifies. Who is he who condemns? It is Christ who died, and furthermore is also risen, who is even at the right hand of God, who also makes intercession for us"* (Romans 8:33-34, KJV).

The mighty God of the Bible is our refuge, our protector. It is to Jesus we must go quietly and quickly for sanctuary when circumstances or thoughts rouse the feelings of fear and dread which tempt us to look inward instead of at our Captain.

Do you fear the Justice of God? You should. But in Christ you are secure and safe. He is our refuge—our only refuge.

The Power of the Lord is Proclaimed: "God is our strength"
Do you fear your own weakness? Maybe you should, but not to the point that you do not obey God and do what He commands. God never asks you to do anything that He does not give you the power to do. He is our power—our strength. If Christ is your strength, then there is absolutely nothing you cannot do if He bids you to do it. Never fear any task or course of action given by the One who is our refuge and strength.

> In His strength, you can face any issue.
> In His strength, you can deal with any problem.
> In His strength you can meet any situation.
> In His strength you can overcome any obstacle.

He gave Moses power over Pharaoh. He gave David power over the giant, Goliath. He gave Elijah power over the false prophets. He gave Paul power over the religious leaders of his day. So why should we fear? His protection is provided and His power is proclaimed.

The Presence of the Lord is Promised: "a very present help in trouble"

God is not distant, uninterested, and uninvolved in our circumstances, but rather a *"very present help."* Our Savior-King promises to be beside us every step of the way through every circumstance of life. Let us not fear! We are called to trust and believe His promise; walk accordingly and your fears will diminish.

As I have indicated before, I grew up in the mountains of Eastern Kentucky and often walked a winding road along the foot hills that dropped off into the river in some places. Sometimes it was pitch black dark when I walked this road at night coming home late from some school event. I remember the fear I had of walking off the edge, stepping on a snake, or of some wild animal lunging at me from the darkness. But when my dad was walking with me, I wasn't afraid of anything. Now, if God is *"a very present help,"* why should His child ever be afraid? Whatever He instructs us to do, wherever He is leading, He is always with us. He has given His word. Feelings will betray reality; He will not abandon His child.

If you are convinced that God Himself is your *protection*, your *power*, and your *ever-present help*, should you fear anything? Notice the Psalmist's conclusion: *"Therefore we will not fear..."* Meditate on those words and believe in Him. If our hearts and minds are filled with the knowledge of His protection, power, and presence, fear will find no place to latch onto and darken our path.

The Permanence of the Promises (vv. 2-3)

Several catastrophic events are listed in Psalm 46. The writer declares that regardless of what may occur, earthquakes, invasions, etc., the Lord is our refuge, strength, and He is always present to help. If we remember that Christ is sovereign and that it is He who sends the catastrophic events into His world, we can be assured that He will care for His own children. We are safe in Him through any circumstance that may come. So why should we fear? Whatever comes from our Father's hand is right and good. His promises are not wavering and shifting; they are unalterable and permanent. All creation serves Him. Men judge on appearances, God sees things in their consequences. Trust Him. Fear Not!

> God moves in a mysterious way,
> His wonders to perform;
> He plants His footsteps in the sea,
> And rides upon the storm. [3]

The Prominent Fear

Common among all people, even the people of God, is the fear of death. I recently read a story about a Catholic priest, a Protestant pastor, and a Jewish rabbi discussing what they desired people to say about them as they lay in their casket for public viewing after their death.

The Catholic priest wanted people to say that he was a righteous, honest, and very generous man. The Protestant pastor said that he wanted people to say that he was kind, fair, and a good pastor to his people. The Jewish rabbi said that he hoped someone would say, "Oh, look! He's moving!"

While this is just a fictitious and humorous story, it does give us some idea about what people think about death and dying. When folks talk about death and dying, they usually avoid talking about their own death. And when speaking about the death of others, they will most often use a euphemism such as "expired" or "passed away." The word "death" or "dead" has a sting to it. It can be the master among terrors. Why is this? Let me suggest a couple of reasons.

First, death is the unknown experience. When we talk of death, we are basically in the area of mystery and darkness. The Bible is, for the most part, silent on the subject of the after-death experience. This unknown aspect about death can create a profitless and sometimes paralyzing fear if not dealt with properly.

Second, death creates fear of the judgment of God. For most people, it's frightening to think of standing before a holy God and giving an account for your life on this earth. This should not be true for the Christian. Christ has fully experienced the penalty for our sins and paid the full price required by Justice. Not only that, but Christ's perfect and righteous life has been credited to us. Because of the work of God the Son, the Christian stands Justified in His sight. Therefore, death is a crossing over to the fullness of eternal life with Him. It is certainly true that we will stand before the Judgement Seat of Christ, to give account of the deeds done in the body, whether good or worthless.

The children of God are to trust in the finished work of Christ knowing that He came to deliver us from the fear of death.

> *Therefore, since the children share in flesh and blood, He Himself likewise also partook of the same, that through death He might render powerless him who had the power of death, that is, the devil, and might free those who through fear of death were subject to slavery all their lives.* (Hebrews 2:14-15)

No true believer should ever fear death. Christ came and conquered death by experiencing it for us. Never allow Satan to rob you of the joy of anticipating being with Christ beyond this life. Certainly we grieve when a believing loved one dies, not because of the fear of death, but because we will miss them, we may fear life without them. However, we do not grieve as those who have no hope (1 Thessalonians 4:13-18). Remember what Paul said: *"to die is gain"* (Philippians 1:21-23).

Besides all this, Paul reminds us that *"Death is swallowed up in victory"* and that the stinger in death has been removed. *"O death where is your victory? O death where is your sting? The sting of death is sin, and the power of sin is the law; but thanks be to God, who gives us the victory through our Lord Jesus Christ"* (1 Corinthians 15:54-57). Through death on Calvary's tree and His resurrection from the grave, Jesus took the stinger out of death.

When I was growing up on our farm in Eastern Kentucky, there was a certain spot on the farm that was always infested with what we called "sand hornets." At times those things would come at you like dive bombers. When my brother and I had to go through "hornet occupied territory" we would run as fast as our legs would carry us. Suppose that in some way we could have removed the stingers from those creatures, would we have been afraid? Of course not! That which caused us to fear was the sting they could inflict; if the stingers were gone there would have been no fear. That's what our Lord did to death: He removed the stinger, He took the sting for us when He paid our sin debt on the Cross. Now we can go through death's territory without fear.

What is it that you are wrestling with in your sleepless nights? What is it that creates restlessness in your life? Circumstances may change, but our God does not; He is the same yesterday, today, and forever. He is still our refuge, strength, and present help in times of need. The Christian has a light that shines in the darkest of times and in the face of the greatest of fears. Christ the King is present with us in the valley of the shadow of death. He commands all; all His commands are good. Fear not!

The great reformer Martin Luther and his companions, with all their boldness and readiness for danger and death in their fight for truth, had times of discouragement and depression and fear. On those occasions, Luther would say to his companions, "Come, let us sing the 46th Psalm," and they would sing Luther's own version:

> A sure stronghold our God is He,
> A timely shield and weapon;
> Our help He'll be, and set us free
> From every ill can happen.
> And were the world with devils filled,
> All eager to devour us
> Our souls to fear shall little yield.
> They cannot overpower us. [4]

Christ Jesus is our refuge: flee to Him, rely upon Him. He is our strength. Look to Him, He is Truth present. If this is true, why fear? Someone has described fear with this little acrostic:

False
Evidence
Appearing
Real

---

1 William Cowper, *Olney Hymnal*, Book III, #15
2 Thomas Watson (1620-1686), www.gracegems.org/6/eternity.htm
3 William Cowper, *Olney Hymnal*, Book III, #15
4 Martin Luther (1483-1546), Redemption Hill Music, redemptionhillmusic.com

13

DEATH

> We spend our years with sighing;
> it is a valley of tears;
> but death is the funeral of all our sorrows. [1]

> Death is only a grim porter to let us into a stately palace. [2]

Legend tells of a Babylonian merchant who sent his servant to the market. Soon the servant returned, white and trembling, and in great agitation said to his master, "Down in the marketplace I was jostled by a woman in the crowd. When I turned around I saw it was Death that jostled me. She looked at me and made a threatening gesture. Master, please lend me your horse, for I must hasten away to avoid her. I will ride to Samara and there I will hide, and Death will not find me."

The merchant lent him a fast horse and the servant galloped away in great haste. Later the merchant went to the marketplace and saw Death standing in the crowd. He went over to her and asked, "Why did you frighten my servant this morning? Why did you make a threatening gesture?"

"That was no threatening gesture," Death replied. "It was only a start of surprise. I was astonished to see him in Baghdad, for I have an appointment with him tonight in Samara."

Do you know what? Each of us has an appointment with death at some certain time and in some certain place, but it doesn't have to be an occasion to fear. If you know the Lord Jesus Christ personally through saving faith, you also know that He holds the key of life and death. As a believer you know that, don't you???

Speaking of man and speaking to the Lord, Job said, *"his days are determined, the number of his months is with You; and his limits You have set so that he cannot pass"* (Job 14:5). The Lord said, *"It is I who puts to death and gives life"* (Deuteronomy 32:39). David, the Psalmist, wrote, *"And in Your book were all written the days that were ordained for me, when as yet there was not one of them"* (Psalm 139:14). You have an appointment with death. But death for the believer is an eternal beginning, not a final end.

Every generation since the Fall of Man has wrestled with questions about death:
    "What is death?"
    "What is it like to die?"
    "What happens after death?"
    "If a man dies, will he live again?" (Job 14:14).

But even with these questions on the minds of people, death is a subject about which few people want to speak, especially their own death. People may joke about death saying such things as, "I hate death, in fact I could live forever without it," or "It's not that I am afraid to die, I just don't want to be there when it happens." And yet another: "Two things everyone must face, taxes and death."

Death, however, is not a joke; death is a fact. As soon as a man starts to live, he is old enough to die. Walk through any cemetery and you'll find the graves of those who lived long lives, those who died in the prime of life, and those whose little hearts had just begun to beat. Each of us has an appointment with death, young or old, *"in-*

asmuch as it is appointed for men to die" (Hebrews 9:27). Wisdom tells us to be prepared for our appointments.

For truth about death, we must look at the textbook on death, the Word of God. There are three kinds of death about which the Word of God speaks: *spiritual death, physical death,* and *eternal death.* There is a common thread associated with each—all result in a form of separation.

Spiritual Death
God created Adam, our Representative, and placed him in the Garden of Eden. From Adam's side God fashioned Eve, the man's wife. The beauty and perfection of Eden was beyond our ability to conceive. It would make any botanical garden anywhere in the world look like kids playing with crayons. It was in this Paradise Creation that God issued His first command to Adam saying, *"From any tree of the garden you may eat freely; but from the tree of the knowledge of good and evil you shall not eat, for in the day that you eat from it you will surely die"* (Genesis 2:16-17).

Did God keep His promise? After all, He did state that if Adam ate of the "tree of the knowledge of good and evil" he would surely die. Scripture tells us that Adam did eat of the tree, but there were no funeral arrangements made for either Adam or his wife Eve. Adam did not die physically for hundreds of years. But that act of rebellion, that evil of choosing a course different than the will of the Creator, ushered in two kinds of death: *spiritual death* and ultimately *physical death.* The moment Adam bit into the fruit from the forbidden tree, he immediately died spiritually. Rather than being the holy man made by the hands of the Creator, Adam became corrupt, a man saturated with sin throughout his being. Light and joy of innocence and fellowship with God instantly turned into darkness and guilt.

Were Adam and Eve conscious of what had happened? Yes! Trying to cover their sinfulness and shame with fig leaves, the couple hid from their Creator. Everything was now different, flawed, corrupted, out of harmony: the universe changed.

When created and placed in the Garden, Adam was the representative of the human race. His obedience or disobedience would affect the entire human race as well as human history. Had Adam not sinned there would have been no death, spiritually or physically. But Adam *did* disobey and *did* die. Every human being has inherited a sinful fallen nature; in Adam all sinned.

> *Therefore, just as through one man sin entered into the world, and death through sin, and so death spread to all men, because all sinned.* (Romans 5:12)

Note the universality of the sinfulness of man: *"so death spread to all men, because all sinned."* We all sinned in Adam, who was our representative. Therefore, all men are under the condemnation of God.

How serious was this spiritual death that took place in the Garden of Eden? That one act of sin resulted in separation from God—a wide and mighty gulf of separation over which man could not reach. In his spiritual death, man had no desire to love and obey the Creator; he now loved only himself. Paul wrote to the church at Ephesus:

> *And you were dead in your trespasses and sins, in which you formerly walked according to the course of this world, according to the prince of the power of the air, of the spirit that is now working in the sons of disobedience. Among them we too all formerly lived in the lusts of our flesh, indulging the desires of the flesh and of the mind, and were by nature children of wrath, even as the rest.* (Ephesians 2:1-3)

This scripture passage graphically describes every fallen man.

> *Spiritually Dead*, dead in trespasses and sins;
> *Disobedient*, ruled by Satan;
> *Depraved*, living in the lusts of the flesh; and
> *Doomed*, by nature the children of wrath.

"Spiritual death" is a vivid and accurate description of separation from God the Creator. The Bible has much more to say on this subject of man's sinfulness and depraved nature resulting from Adam's disobedience as our representative (Romans 3:9-18, Ephesians 4:17-19). Through the prophet Isaiah God speaks to us, *"Your iniquities have made a separation between you and your God, and your sins have hidden His face from you so that He does not hear"* (Isaiah 59:2).

Physical Death
There is separation involved in physical death as well. There is a separation of the material (the body) and the immaterial (the spirit and or soul). Physical death is the separation of the temporal from the eternal part of man. When God created Adam from the dust of the earth, Adam was just as lifeless as any other piece of dirt. Man became a living being when God breathed into Adam's nostrils the breath of life. That *breath of life* gave and sustained the life of the body of Adam. When that is separated from man, he goes back to the ground from which he was taken. In physical death, the eternal part of man is separated from the body. The body is dead and returns to dust. The eternal part of man was created to be just that, Eternal. Everyone is going to live forever somewhere: eternally *with God* or eternally separated *from God*.

The Bible uses four words to describe physical death. These words give insight and help us to comprehend that coming appointment at the end of our earthly life.

First, *Sleep* is used to describe death. In John 14 is the record of the fascinating story of Lazarus, who died and was raised from the dead by Christ. When Lazarus, the brother of Mary and Martha, became sick, they sent word to Jesus. Instead of rushing to where Lazarus was, Jesus tarried for two days and then announced to His disciples that, *"Our friend Lazarus has fallen asleep, but I go, so that I may awaken him out of sleep"* (John 11:11). The disciples were puzzled and said that if Lazarus was asleep he could recover on his own. Then Jesus told them plainly; Lazarus was dead (John 14:14).

Another example is related to the stoning and death of Stephen in Acts 7:60: *"He fell asleep."*

The word *sleep*, which is used in these passages as a euphemism for death, does not suggest a state of unconsciousness. For the Christian to be *"absent from the body and to be at home with the Lord"* (2 Corinthians 5:8) is not a state of unconsciousness. At the point of death we will be face to face with Jesus our Lord, no separation at all, with Him to enjoy Him forever! But for the unbeliever the opposite: separation forever, condemned forever, payment exacted in hell. Forever! (Luke 16:19-31)

Sleep, for the believer, is quiet rest. At death God delivers his people from life's toils, fears, and trials. Heaven will be a place of rest from all sin. Nothing will be there to spoil or mar or disturb. When I was about six or seven years old, I went with my father to a revival meeting, which was about sixty miles away. In those days, the roads in eastern Kentucky were rough, narrow, and winding, up and down and around the mountains. It didn't take long for me to become very tired. By the time the service was over that night and we started back home, I was exhausted and lay down in the back seat of the car. When I awoke, we were home. Death may be something like that trip I took with my dad. We'll fall asleep here and wake up at home in His presence.

There is one common theme revealed in the ancient burial grounds from the pyramids of Egypt to the burial grounds of Mexico—they all believed in life after death. In a sense they looked on death as sleep, but certainly not in the same way a Christian does.

The second word used for death is *Departure*. Paul expressed death as departure on two occasions.

> *But I am hard-pressed from both directions,*
> *having the desire to depart and be with Christ,*
> *for that is very much better.*
> (Philippians 1:23)

> *For I am already being poured out as a drink offering,*
> *and the time of my departure has come.*
> (2 Timothy 4:6)

The word *depart* means "to unloose, undo, to break up" etc. It is used to refer to the unyoking of an animal from a plow or wagon. When the day's work was done, the owner unloosened, set-free, his animal from its burden so it could rest. This is what Paul has in mind: "I am ready to be unloosed from my burden here on earth and enter my rest there in the presence of the Lord."

Depart was also utilized to describe the freeing of a prisoner from his chains, stocks, or dungeon. Those things were very real to Paul, who was in a Roman jail when he wrote the letter to the church at Philippi. No doubt he was thinking about an exchange of prison in Rome for the glories and liberties of heaven. A glorious departure!

Further, *depart* was used when referring to the loosing of the mooring ropes of a ship so it could set sail. Paul had seen this many times in his travels, and now He wanted to be loosed from this earthly harbor to set sail for heaven.

A third word referring to death is *dissolve*, meaning to strike or tear down. It is a graphic word describing death for the believer. Paul wrote:

> *For we know that if the earthly tent which is our house is torn down,* [dissolved or struck down] *we have a building from God, a house not made with hands, eternal in the heavens.* (2 Corinthians 5:1, parenthesis mine)

The meaning is to fold up a tent and set it aside. Paul compared our bodies to a tent. A tent is not a permanent dwelling place; it is temporary and so are our bodies. Being a tentmaker by trade, Paul was very familiar with this truth. So when he thought about death, he saw it as simply taking down and folding up and laying aside a worn out tent, which was only temporary, and moving into a new and permanent dwelling place: Home. He saw death as moving out of the old tent and moving in with the King, into His palace of glory. Christ prepares a dwelling place made especially for His children; an inheritance is ours—permanent, an ever-brightening eternity with Him.

With every passing day, especially when it's time to get out of bed in the morning, I am made painfully aware that this body, this earthly tent, is wearing out and will soon have to be struck and folded up and laid aside. Then I'll move in with the King.

> When John Quincy Adams was 80 years old, a friend met him on a street in Boston and asked, "How is John Quincy Adams today?" The former U.S. President replied, "John Quincy Adams himself is well, quite well, I thank you. But the house in which he lives at present is becoming quite dilapidated. It is teetering upon its foundation. Time and seasons have

> nearly destroyed it. Its roof is pretty well worn out; its walls are much shattered and tremble with every wind. The old tenement is becoming almost uninhabitable, and I think John Quincy Adams will have to move out of it soon. But he himself is quite well, quite well!" [3]

The aged sixth President of the United States President was about ready to fold up his tent and move to a permanent dwelling with his Lord. He died at age 81.

And fourth, there is yet another word used for death, *Deceased*. On the mount of transfiguration, when Moses and Elijah were discussing the death of Christ, they spoke of His decease (Luke 9:31, NKJV). Later other translations used the word "death" or "departure." The word means "an exodus" or "a going out." The word finds its roots and significance in the Old Testament "Exodus." The Exodus was a going out from bondage to blessings.

What a beautiful metaphor for the Christian. Death for them is going out of Egypt (the world) into the very presence of God! That's what Death is for the Child of God—from gloom to glory. We are in the land of the dying on our way to the land of the living. At death we can say, "I have been dying all my days; now I am going to live." It is like weighing anchor and sailing for the Glorious Land, or laying aside a worn out tent and moving into the splendor of the King's palace, or like taking our exodus from Egypt (the world) and going to the Celestial City.

Is it any wonder that Paul could say, *"For to me, to live is Christ and to die is gain...I am hard-pressed from both directions, having the desire to depart and be with Christ, for that is very much better"* (Philippians 1:21, 23). These are not the words of a bitter grouchy old man who is fed up with life and wanted to die. He was not saying that death had become the lesser of two evils (living or dying), but that dying was the greater blessing. Life was good for Paul, but to depart and be with Christ was far better.

Life does not end at the cemetery—there is life beyond and we get there through the door of death. For the Christian, life with Christ is a life of joy, peace, fullness, glory, and bliss. But for the unbeliever, it is only the beginning of endless regrets and torments; death for them **should** be frightening.

Eternal Death
Every one of Adam's descendants is born dead *spiritually*; every one, except those alive at His Second Coming will die *physically*; not everyone will die *eternally*. Eternal death also involves a separation: an eternal separation from God, from all that He is except His holy wrath against sin. It is separation from the love, grace, mercies, joys, security, and hopes that can only be found in a saving relationship with Christ the Lord. When a person dies without this relationship, the only prospect is the unfettered wrath of God for eternity and separation from all that is good and right. In Scripture this is called *"the second death"* (Revelation 20:6, 14), because it follows physical death.

Every person is going to live forever somewhere. Scripturally there are only two alternatives: Heaven or Hell. The question is: IN WHICH PLACE WILL YOU SPEND ETERNITY? I have somewhere read that in an Indiana cemetery a tombstone was found which reads:

> Pause, stranger, when you pass me by;
> As you are now, so once was I,
> As I am now, so you will be,
> So prepare for death and follow me.

Then someone came by the grave, read the epitaph, and wrote below it:

> To follow you I'm not content,
> Until I know which way you went.

You may have smiled as you read the above, but there's some truth in those messages. Wherever you spend eternity, the reality of it will begin as soon as you die physically. The rich man in Luke 16 found out in an instant what it was to be separated from God in the eternal torments of hell. On the other hand, the Apostle Paul expressed the expectation of the Christian: *"We are of good courage, I say, and prefer rather to be absent from the body and to be at home with the Lord"* (2 Corinthians 5:8). *"For me, to live is Christ and to die is gain..."* (Philippians 1:21).

The body of the child of God will physically die, but that which is eternal is with the Lord who loved him and redeemed him. When Christ returns, the eternal part of those who love Christ will unite with new glorified bodies. We will then—without end—forever—live in the conscious and physical presence of the Lord.

For the unbeliever, he too will be united with his body and come forth from the grave, but then he will be judged and cast into outer darkness, separated from the Lord eternally.

I once read a story about a physician who was also a Bible teacher and preacher. The story goes that, after speaking one day, he was confronted by an atheist who said, "I don't believe a word you're preaching." The good doctor replied, "Well now, you've told me what you *don't* believe; perhaps you can tell me what you *do* believe." "I believe that death ends all," replied the atheist. "I too believe that," responded the doctor. Startled, the atheist responded, "What! You believe death ends all?"

The doctor continued, "I most certainly do believe death ends all. It will end all your chances to do evil; it will end all your aspirations in life; all your plans and all your friendships. But most of all, your death will be the end of all chances of you ever again hearing the gospel of the redeeming grace of God in Christ. You will go into outer darkness."

"But for me, death ends all my disappointments in life; all my tears over sorrow and sin; and all my pain and suffering. Yes sir, all that will end for me and I will depart this life to be with My Lord." Stunned, the atheist replied, "I never thought of it that way." In the conversation that ensued, the doctor was, by God's grace, able to lead the man to Christ.

After having been quiet and silent for a lengthy time, the aged and feeble Charles Wesley, the great hymn writer, called Mrs. Wesley to him, and requested her to write the following lines at his direction:

> In age and feebleness extreme,
> Who shall a sinful world redeem?
> Jesus, my only hope thou art,
> Strength of my failing flesh and heart
> O could I catch a smile from thee,
> And drop into eternity. [4]

D.L. Moody used to tell this story: During the last war a young man lay on a cot, and they heard him say, "Here!" Someone went to his cot and heard the injured man say, "Hark! Hush! Don't you hear them? They are calling the roll in heaven." He lifted his head slightly and said, "Here!"—And he was gone.

> Here on earth—we find a mixture of evil in our best moments! When we approach nearest to God, we

have the quickest sense of our defilement, and how much we fall short in every branch of duty, and in every temper of our hearts. But when we shall see Jesus as He is—we shall be fully transformed into His image, and be perfectly like Him! [5]

Yes dear friends, we are already God's children, and we can't even imagine what we will be like when Christ returns. But we do know that when He comes—"we will be made like Him, for we will see Him as He really is!" (1 John 3:2)

---

1 Thomas Watson (1620-1686), www.savedbygracesuicidenetwork.org/other_side.htm
2 Richard Sibbs (1577-1635), www.jonathanemason.com/p.247
3 John Q. Adams, *The Meaning of Faith*, Harry Emerson Fosdick, Association Press, 1922, p. 71
4 Charles Wesley (1707-1788), www.wholesomewords.org/biography/bwesley6.html
5 John Newton, *The Works of John Newton, Volume 2*, Hamilton, Adams, and Co., 1820, reprinted by Banner of Truth Trust, 1988, pg. 476-477

14

GRIEF

Grief is itself a medicine. [1]

That were a grief I could not bear,
Didst Thou not hear and answer prayer.
But a prayer-hearing, answering God,
Supports me under every load. [2]

Earnest Hemingway said, "All stories, if continued far enough, end in death, because life ends in death." [3] As we have seen in the last chapter, death is inevitable; how we face and deal with the death of a loved one says a great deal about our trust in the Lord and the depth of our submission to His will.

In our last chapter we talked about the death of both believers and unbelievers. The Bible describes death for the believer as *sleep, departure, dissolving,* and *exodus*. But, after a death, Grief comes like a dark horse bearing us downward into unknown places. Heartache and sorrow in grief may arise from many events: loss of job, divorce, physical injury, etc., but this chapter focuses primarily on grief associated with death.

How LONG Does Grief Last?
The length of time one grieves after the loss of a loved one varies; the ride on grief's dark horse down shadowy valleys is different for each person. Grief is not on a schedule that you can rush. The process may be almost unbearably painful. Even so, grief has to take its own course for each individual. Some may recover quite rapidly, but

for others the emotions of missing that person may last for the rest of their life. This does not mean that the agony and pain experienced at first will last that long. The average healing process for grieving is about five years. Again, this does not mean that you will have forgotten that loved one at the end of five years, but the major process of grieving will probably be ended. The darkness of sorrow will not last forever for the Christian. But be aware, it is normal for the old emotions of grief to arise on significant dates, birthdays, and holidays. Even certain smells can trigger deep memories.

> Death leaves a heartache no one can heal,
> Love leaves a memory none can steal. [4]

EMOTIONS and Grief
When Susan, my little girl, was killed, many loving and well-meaning people tried to console me by saying that they knew how I felt. As concerned and well-intended their words were, they didn't really discern what state of mind I was in and where I was in the grief process. I received many letters from people from different parts of the country who did not say that they knew how I felt; all they did was tell me about the loss of their child and I immediately knew these folks had ridden that same dark steed through DarkLand. They understood quite well what the grieving process was. So, let's discuss some of the emotions associated with deep and personal broken-heartedness after the death of a loved one. Keep in mind, these emotions may vary with each individual. The path in this part of DarkLand is well-worn and always in use.

The first emotion one may experience upon the knowledge of the death of a loved one is *Shock*. This is especially true if it is the sudden death of a close family member: wife, husband, son, daughter, father, or mother. There's a numbness that cascades over you, overwhelming in its depth and power. It's almost a sensation that says, "This is not real but a dream." How can it be that this has happened?

You hope you can wake up and find that it *was* all a dream. This condition can last for a few hours or sometimes days. I remember well this very experience when the police officer knocked on my door and informed me that my daughter was dead. At this point, my mind was flooded with questions. Our questions may never be answered until the Lord Himself answers them face to face.

We descend the path and the dark horse pauses on a ledge called *Regret*. It's not uncommon when a loved one dies for the remaining family and close friends to begin searching for answers. They sometimes go on a guilt trip which triggers a cruel "if only" game. "If only" I had done this or "if only" I had not done that, they may not have died. Guilt may even start a "should have" game. "I should have done this" or "I should have done that." These are natural tendencies, but the grieving Christian must not stop here; turn away from the *ledge of Regret* and look in the direction of the King, move forward and begin the healing process which will probably necessitate traveling through rugged and difficult terrain. Grief manifests itself in different and unusual ways, and the stricken heart will almost always pass through a number of places on the way up and out in this painful journey.

Anxiety may be especially powerful when a husband or wife dies, and to a deeper degree if the grieving spouse was totally dependent on the other. This is often found when a husband of a long time marriage dies. He has taken care of all the finances and taxpaying, all of the house repairs, all the lawn care, all car upkeep, and perhaps most of the driving. The grieving widow often finds herself completely overwhelmed with the burdens of running the household in the absence of her husband. She may be uncertain and anxious about her own welfare: "who will take care of me now?"

Some people find themselves taken deeper and deeper into uncharted territory—the yawning pits of *Depression*. Depression is that midnight of the soul that settles when death takes a loved one. You feel that the sun will never shine in your life again. I suspect that depression, *to some degree*, is the experience of every person who has lost someone very close and beloved to them, especially a husband, wife, or child. If you are a believer, you begin to realize that this death represents a long separation from that loved one. You may wonder if this darkness and painful state of mind are going to last forever. If not overcome, a giant of DarkLand, *Despair*, throws on his chains and shackles; feelings of endless sorrow and hopelessness engulf the mind, obscuring light. And in this terrain there are so many false signposts that say "THIS WILL NEVER END," "THERE'S NO NEED PRESSING FORWARD," "THERE'S NO FUTURE EXCEPT MISERY."

Most people, at one time or another, fall into *self-pity*. When someone close to us dies we are prone to cry out "why me?" or "it's not fair." These are actually expressions of self-pity. In reality when someone who is a Christian dies, our grief and sorrow is for ourselves. They have gone to be with the Lord and we grieve for ourselves because we will miss them; a void is left that none but God can fill. But to wish them back from the presence of the Lord would be very selfish.

Some may begin to look for something in their life that they may conclude caused God to judge them by taking their loved one away. This too is another form of self-pity. It's the attitude of "why are you doing this to me Lord?" This is not far from depression. I think that it would be very rare that the Lord would take a loved one home because of the sin of another. Perhaps David is one case where this did happen. (2 Samuel 12)

Bitterness is another common reaction to death or great loss. Bitterness, resentment, and anger are common expressions of grief, although totally unjustified. These emotions may be directed at any number of people: a family member, physician, or even the Lord. Bitterness expresses itself by an attitude that demands that someone pay, and that will add resentment on top of the bitterness, revealing itself by agitation toward family members, fellow workers, church family…

Mixed emotions. Sometimes death may be a welcome relief. When death comes to a loved one who, because of some disease or injury, has endured intense and long term pain, the family who has cared for them may be both physically and emotionally drained. Having seen a loved one suffering and knowing that there is no hope of recovery, the family often experiences emotions of relief and thankfulness when death comes to the one they love so much. Mixed in with those emotions may be a form of guilt that creeps in for being thankful that their suffering is over and death has come. Mixed emotions—relief, guilt, and regret.

If you are grieving, don't be surprised if you sometimes feel as though you are "going crazy," you think people do not understand you, you become easily irritated or nervous, or you want to escape; guilt and remorse fill your heart, and you are unable to focus. These are normal reactions, but cannot be permitted to persist. If allowed and rehearsed again and again, there follows a spiral into discouragement and even depression. In a letter to a grieving widow, John Newton not only consoled and wept with her, but also gave the following counsel:

> Your wound while fresh, is painful; but faith, prayer, and time, will, I trust, gradually render it tolerable. There is something quite strange about grief; painful

> as it is, we are prone to indulge it, and to brood over the thoughts and circumstances which are suited (like fuel to fire) to heighten and prolong it...Grief, when indulged and excessive, preys upon the spirits, injures health, indisposes us for duty, and causes us to shed tears, which deserve more tears. [5]

All the emotions we have discussed—*shock, anxiety, depression, regret, self-pity, bitterness,* and *mixed emotions*—are somewhat normal for a grieving person. So you can expect a knock on your door from them when you are in a state of grief, but you don't have to invite them in, feed them, and make them your bosom friend. If not dealt with they can destroy you. Even the believer is drained and weakened; only the great King can wield the sword that cuts away any shackles of despair and lead us upward to Himself.

As common and normal as grief is, if you are not delivered from it in a reasonable period of time, it will destroy you. We must handle grief or it will handle us. So, from my own experience of dealing with grief, the following are eight suggestions on handling grief.

1. Turn to the Lord. Paul reminds us, *"Blessed be the God and Father of our Lord Jesus Christ, the Father of mercies and God of all comfort, who comforts us in all our affliction..."* (2 Corinthians 1:3-4). He is blessed because He is *"the Father of mercies, and God of all comfort."* He comforts because He is merciful, He "fortifies" us. That is what the word "comfort" means. He encircles us with love and encouragement and protection. He strengthens us so we can face the emotions of grief with new determination and faith.

No one can comfort like He does. He knows your every weakness and your every strength. He knows where to supply strength and encouragement for your grieving wounded heart. He may do that through another person who has gone through the process of grieving themselves. However He may choose to do it, He is the source of all comfort for those who grieve.

2. Accept death as a part of our existence. Death is as much a part of us as birth and growth. The atheist George Bernard Shaw was right when he said, "Life's ultimate statistic is the same for all, one out of one dies." [6] Death is inevitable for every person unless you are living when the Lord returns; even then, there will take place a sort of death experience when we are changed into His likeness—death of the old, life eternal.

Only when you begin to acknowledge death as a part of your existence and accept that your loved one is gone, will you begin to recover. Denial fades away and reality can be faced.

3. Express your grief. Tears are a natural way to express grief. Tear ducts are God's pressure valves through which grief is released by flowing tears. When I was growing up on the farm in eastern Kentucky, my mother had a pressure cooker. This cooker was used to can vegetables in those old canning jars. The vegetables were put into jars, sealed with a lid, placed in a pressure cooker, and then heated to a very high temperature. If the pressure got too severe, the pop-off valve on the cooker would pop open to allow the pressure to escape so the cooker wouldn't explode. The valve on the cooker is somewhat like our tear ducts, releasing the pressure in our souls.

Unfortunately, in the midst of grief, some well-meaning person may say, "You've got to keep your chin up; you've got to be brave; after all, tears are a sign of a weak faith." That's rubbish! The Bible instructs us to, *"Weep with them that weep"* (Romans 17:15); Paul, a man's man, added: *"I wrote to you with many tears"* (2 Corinthians 2:4).

The God who gave you a nose for smelling, ears for hearing, eyes for seeing, and a mouth for eating, smiling, and talking also gave you tear ducts for weeping. Fighting back tears does not relieve sorrow nor will it remove grief. Weep when you feel like weeping. Tears are part of God's healing process.

4. Live through your memories. Again some well-meaning person may say to you, "O! You must forget about the past and start a new life." That's not good advice, even if you could do it. Don't run from memories of your loved one—live through them, because as the old song says, "They will ever flood your soul."

Listen to familiar music, look through pictures, wear familiar clothes, shop in familiar places, sit in favorite chairs, etc. The adjustment must be made in the place the grief was inflicted. You cannot run from death and you cannot run from grief.

Handling the clothing and personal things of the deceased may be a little painful, but it is necessary. When Dorcas died, her friends wept as they viewed the garments she had made for them (Acts 9:39).

Don't be hurried into decision making. There will be plenty of time to make decisions when grief subsides and you can think more clearly.

5. Talk out your feelings. Express your sorrow and grief not only with tears, but in words as well. Verbalize your feelings to someone whom you trust and are confident will be a good listener and not so quick to give advice. This can be a family member, a dear friend, or your pastor.

6. Stay busy. If you don't already have a hobby, find one you can enjoy. You can find things to do in the church, or you can start a needed ministry in your church, ministering to the shut-ins, visiting the sick, etc. The idea is to get involved with people doing things.

When King David's baby lay sick, David isolated himself in grief. He wept, he fasted, and prayed, but when the child died, David went first to worship God, then plunged back into the responsibilities of leading his people (2 Samuel 12:20). Idleness will only increase your propensity to become bitter, depressed, confused, angry, and wallowing in self-pity.

7. *Exercise and eat properly.* It is important that you exercise the body to keep the blood flowing properly and to keep your muscles toned. Inactivity will weaken the body and leave the mind vulnerable. Exercising is good for the mind; as you get your heart rate up, the blood flows and your thinking will be more normal. Eating nutritious foods will enhance your ability to exercise properly and your recovery time will be shortened.

8. *Think of life as a gift from God.* Whatever time God gives you to enjoy another person in your life, that person is a precious gift from God. Sometimes in marriage that person may be with you for many years. However at other times that gift may be short lived. My daughter was only eleven years of age when she died, but she was such a joy and precious gift even though she lived a short life. When Job's entire family was taken from him in death, he said: *"The Lord gave and the Lord has taken away. Blessed be the name of the Lord"* (Job 1:21). Job expresses the very attitude we should have when we lose a loved one. This will not stop the grief, but it sure will shorten the worst of it.

When the tornado is coming, it is too late to plan a storm shelter. When you are awakened by smoke and flames in your home, it is too late to purchase fire insurance. So obviously the time to prepare for the unexpected events in your life, including death, is to prepare before they come. If you build on the rock of God's Word and His Son today, then you can stand firm in the times when troubles flood over your soul. They are coming.

Talk to family and friends, be involved in your church, eat good foods, take time to relax, listen to your favorite music, and be patient with yourself. Focus on Christ the Great Physician and the Good, Great, and Chief Shepherd.

Comfort Those Who Grieve
I have never, in my more than fifty years in service to the Lord, met the person who does not need ministering to when they lose a loved one. When death takes someone we love, we experience powerful emotions associated with loss and grief.

Friends can play a vital part in the recovery process. Life is not meant to be lived as a solo, but as a chorus. The Bible instructs us to help one another through the hard times of life: *"Bear one another's burdens"* (Galatians 6:2). *"Now we who are strong ought to bear the weaknesses of those without strength"* (Romans 15:1). *"Rejoice with those who rejoice, and weep with those who weep"* (Romans 12:15). A loving friend can bring a little light to the dark of grieving. The lamp that sheds light on our path may be held by the hand of a friend.

Christ Jesus set before us the great example of how to minister to the grieving (John 11:1-44). He was on a preaching mission when word came to Him that Lazarus, His friend, was critically ill. By the time Jesus arrived at Bethany where Lazarus and his sisters, Mary and Martha, lived, Lazarus was already dead and had been buried for four days. Hearing that Jesus was coming, Martha ran to meet Him and said:

> *"Lord, if You had been here, my brother would not have died. Even now I know that whatever You ask of*

> *God, God will give You." Jesus said to her, "Your brother will rise again." Martha said to Him, "I know that he will rise again in the resurrection on the last day." Jesus said to her, "I am the resurrection and the life; he who believes in Me will live even if he dies, and everyone who lives and believes in Me will never die. Do you believe this?" She said to Him, "Yes, Lord; I have believed that You are the Christ, the Son of God, even He who comes into the world."* (John 11:21-27)

Jesus went to the grave of Lazarus and commanded the stone be removed from the entrance. When the stone was removed, Jesus shouted, *"Lazarus, come forth!"* (v. 43). Immediately, the voice of the Creator God was obeyed; Lazarus came forth from death's grip, alive and restored.

In this event, Jesus did four things. *First, Jesus WENT to where Lazarus was* (John 11:17). He went to be with the sorrowing family. Don't call on the phone if you can possibly go. That is the first thing we ought to do when we want to give comfort. I can almost hear someone thinking, "But I feel so inadequate. I don't know what to say." We all feel helpless in these difficult circumstances. I've been visiting people in their grief for more than fifty years and I still feel inadequate.

I finally learned that it isn't always necessary to say something. A heart broken by grief and loss needs your concern and love, not a sermon, simple answers, and scripture quotations. Your personal presence and assurance of your prayers are of more value than words alone could ever be.

A caring touch, a warm handclasp, a loving pat on the shoulder, or a tender embrace—these actions speak an inaudible and powerful language of their own. And a sorrowing mind needs a sympathetic ear to verbalize their grief.

Don't ask your grieving friend if there is anything you can do, but rather ask that question of a relative, or look for things that need to be done: answer the phone, greet friends at the door, take care of the small children, do washing, ironing, cooking, cut grass, run errands.

Second, Jesus WEPT with the family (v. 35). Don't restrain your own tears, which come naturally; your grieving friend will see your love and concern. Your grief may encourage them to express their own grief. Jesus wept with Mary and Martha. He entered into their sorrow. He wept and allowed them to weep.

Be the kind of friend that the grieving person is not ashamed to weep before. That means that they have to know that you are hurting with them. The old stoic attitude usually gets the most praise from the well-meaning, but mistaken friends. "Oh, you're being so brave," "you're taking it so well," "how wonderful you are, not letting this get you down." This is not the best way to deal with a heart in pain and grief; they need to weep tears to release the pent up emotions. Jesus wept; you do the same. *"Weep with those who weep"* (Romans 12:15).

Third, Jesus WITNESSED to them (vs. 23-26). He gave hope and assurance for the future. He told Martha that her brother would rise again. Then He told her an amazing thing, namely, that He Himself is the Resurrection and the Life. This is not some impersonal idea or declaration. Christ is the Resurrection because He is the very source and power of life. He gives life and He takes life. What a comfort this was to Martha. Yes, Lazarus her brother was dead, but the Resurrection and Life was present. Yes, we should share our friend's sorrow, but we must share our Savior as well. *When the time is right* we must gently point them to Christ the Lord and King for comfort and strength.

The best witness is one of experience. Some of Richard Baxter's (author of a book on death) preacher friends criticized him for grieving too long over the death of his wife. Mr. Baxter's reply was, "I will not be judged by those who have never known the like." Those who have walked through the dark valley of grief can best lead a grieving friend through that valley and into the Sonlight.

When the time is right, we can give witness to the lost person who is grieving, and we can give comfort to the child of God. Again, personal testimonies of how God has rescued you and made you His own or how His grace has sustained and comforted you through sorrow and grief can give comfort. Sometimes when a person has lost a loved one, they are more open to the gospel than at any other time. Death awakens, sobers, and challenges the living.

The fourth thing Jesus did was to WAKE Lazarus from the dead (vs.43-44). We certainly cannot raise the dead, but we can without doubt give assurances to the Christian that that body will someday come forth from the grave more alive than before they died.

Let me say this again: when storm clouds gather and the lightning strikes, it is too late to plan a storm shelter. When you awaken to flames in your home, it is too late to arrange for that fire insurance you've been meaning to buy. The time to prepare for events is before they come to pass. The time to build your spiritual foundation is now. If you build on the rock of God's Word and His Son Jesus Christ today, then you can stand in times of trouble and darkness. While we are mourning the loss of a loved one *here*, there are others rejoicing at their arrival *there*. Lay all grief at the foot of the throne of the One who *"bore our griefs, and carried our sorrows"* (Isaiah 53:4).

> God of my life, to Thee I call,
> Afflicted at Thy feet I fall;
> When the great water-floods prevail,
> Leave not my trembling heart to fail.
>
> Friend of the friendless and the faint,
> Where should I lodge my deep complaint?
> Where but with Thee, whose open door
> Invites the helpless and the poor!
>
> Did ever mourner plead with Thee,
> And Thou refuse that mourner's plea?
> Does not the word still fixed remain,
> That none shall seek Thy face in vain?
>
> That were a grief I could not bear,
> Did'st Thou not hear and answer prayer.
> But a prayer-hearing, answering God,
> Supports me under every load.
>
> Fair is the lot that's cast for me;
> I have an Advocate with Thee;
> They whom the world caresses most,
> Have no such privilege to boast.
>
> Poor tho' I am, despised, forgot,
> Yet God, my God, forgets me not;
> And He is safe, and must succeed,
> For whom the Lord vouchsafes to plead. [7]

1 William Cowper, *Poems by William Cowper of the Inner Temple, ESQ*, printed for J. Johnson, London, 1782, p. 188
2 William Cowper, *Olney Hymnal*, Book III, #19
3 Earnest Hemingway, dchieftain.com
4 www.connollyhospital.ie/en/downloads (on a headstone in Ireland)
5 John Newton, *Cardiphonia*, Morgan and Scott LD, 1911, p. 248-249
6 Joni Erickson Tada, *Nigel M. de S. Cameron*, 2006, p. 224
7 William Cowper, *Olney Hymnal*, Book III #19

15

ANGER

> For embittering life, for breaking communities, for destroying the most sacred relationships, for devastating homes, for withering up men and women, for taking the bloom off childhood, in short, for sheer gratuitous misery-producing power, this influence [Anger] stands alone. [1]

Years ago there was a popular television series about a scientist who on occasions would experience a "sci-fi" sized metamorphose, transforming into a huge green muscular monster, popping buttons and splitting his shirt as he transformed. Remember him? "The Incredible Hulk"! Do you recall what triggered the chilling transformation? It was ANGER!

In some ways the Bible depicts the angry person as a monster. Anger can produce a form of metamorphose in countenance, personality, and emotions; people can become monsters when controlled by anger. Might I even say, in that moment of anger, a person may be in a state of temporary insanity?

Why have a chapter in this book devoted to Anger? A fair question, and here's the answer—the **Bible** speaks of anger well over 1000 times. Any subject given that much attention by Scripture is a serious topic.

Anger gives birth to a host of children. I'll bet you've met them personally. Some of them are malice, hatred, bitterness, resentment, and vengeance. Paul wrote, *"Let all bitterness and wrath and anger and clamor and slander be put away from you, along with all malice."* The opposite is, *"Be kind to one another, tender hearted, forgiving each other, just as God in Christ also has forgiven you"* (Ephesians. 4:31-32).

Anger is an emotional gun: very useful for what it was designed for, but deadly when wrongly used. Anger is an acid that can do more harm to the vessel in which it is stored than on anyone on whom it is poured. It damages all good emotions. Two Christian psychiatrists, Paul Meyer and Frank Minirith, stated that "pent up anger is probably the leading cause of death." [2] Uncontrolled anger is a contorted fiend, destroying the body, relationships, and spiritual health. Anger is like fire: when it finally dies out, it leaves behind a path of destruction. Anger-intoxication reveals one's real character to others but hides itself and justifies itself within the heart that spawns it.

> It is only our bad temper that we put down to being tired or worried or hungry; we put our good temper down to ourselves. [3]

All anger is not bad. Scripture says, *"be angry and sin not"* (Ephesians 4:26). As Christians we want to know what that means. Matthew Henry wrote,

> If we would be angry and not sin...we must be angry at nothing but sin; and we should be more jealous for the glory of God than for any interest or reputation of our own. [4]

We have to be very careful to direct anger at the right object, at the right time, in the right way.

So what is anger? Anger is a feeling of extreme displeasure, hostility, indignation, or exasperation toward someone or something. These are experiences we all have at one time or another. I get angry. You get angry. But in order to avoid admitting that we are angry, we have developed some euphemisms for anger. We like to say that we are irritated, frustrated, exasperated, annoyed, or up-tight, but OH, NO! certainly not angry. Most anger is sinful, and we don't want to be guilty of sin, so we just substitute another word.

Anger, a restless vandal, shows itself by varied ways and plunders our peace and distracts us from the right path. To more easily recognize its many subtleties, let's give them personal names.

There is *Nikita Khrushchev Actor*. You have probably seen him in action. When he doesn't get his way, Nikita becomes angry, slams doors, pounds on tables with his shoes, and stamps his feet. When anyone or anything comes between him and his desires, his selfishness and 'quick to explode' temper take the stage. He reacts like a child in most adult situations.

Meet *Jack Historian*. Old Jack never lets an issue die. He carries a mental shovel and digs up old buried problems and reminds you of them. He has a storage silo where he stockpiles every word and every act in which he thinks he's been wronged; he has them ready and available for recall on the spur of the moment. Jack Historian has an unforgiving heart that erupts in anger. When angry he is in a dangerous state. Christ said, *"if you do not forgive others, then your Father will not forgive your transgressions"* (Matthew 6:15). Could it be that an unforgiving heart is an unforgiven heart?

You know *Mrs. Truthy Teller*, don't you? She always tells the truth (as she sees it, of course). She might remind you of things like how the wrinkles are increasing on your face or how your hair is getting grayer by the day. Of course, she would not pass up an opportunity to tell you how "sorry" she was to hear folks talking about your child's latest failures. Mrs. Truthy Teller is bitter and full of vengeance. She lashes out by pointing out flaws and relating gossip which she perceives will upset you. This is anger in disguise.

Don't forget about *Patricia Put-Down*. Here's how she expresses her deep-seated anger: "Hi, Sarah! Great to see you! You've gained a little weight, haven't you, but you still look good!" And she can say it with a smile on her face. She relishes sticking you with her prickly put-downs. Often this is no more than Patricia's jealousy and resentment growing out of a heart of embedded anger.

Then there is *Old Man Teaser*. You can't forget him even if you try. He pokes fun and laughs about the misfortunes of others. He does the same thing as does *Patricia Put-Down*, except he pretends to be "only joking"; it is still a manifestation of a heart steeped in anger.

> *Like a madman who throws firebrands, arrows and death,*
> *So is the man who deceives his neighbor and says,*
> *"Was I not joking?"*
> (Proverbs 26:18-19)

How about *Linda Slipper*, have you met her? You have undoubtedly seen her in action. She delights in letting little things slip, then pretends to be sorry. She might say something like this, "Did you know that John got fired from his job? But please don't tell anyone you heard it from me, no one is supposed to know about it." She'll pull your heart out and say, "Did I do that?" Anger!

We cannot forget *Greta Gossip*. Everyone has known her or has been her. She's been around for a long time. She never spews her slander and poison unless it is "necessary and informative," of course! Greta is an unhappy, insecure, angry gossip with a tongue set on fire from hell itself, scorching her victim and whoever gives a listening ear. Be careful! See the quote from the book of James below.

In addition to all the above, there are still others. How about *Mr. Blamer, Mrs. Pouter, Mr. Comedian, Miss Rebellious, Mr. Religious,* and who can stand before *Jealousy Greene?* All are anger in veiled disguises with many masks. I listened to an interview with a famous comedian and was surprised when he said that his comedy was only a cover up for anger long held inside since being abused as a child.

You can readily see that the tongue with which man speaks is a powerful instrument of the body, especially when used in anger. A sharp tongue is the only tool that grows sharper with constant use. James wrote this about the tongue:

> *The tongue is a small part of the body, and yet it boasts of great things. See how great a forest is set aflame by such a small fire! And the tongue is a fire, a very world of iniquity; the tongue is set among our members as that which defiles the entire body, and sets on fire the course of our life, and is set on fire by hell. For every species of beasts and birds, of reptiles and creatures of the sea, is tamed and has been tamed by the human race. But no one can tame the tongue; it is a restless evil and full of deadly poison. With it we bless our Lord and Father, and with it we curse men, who have been made in the likeness of God; from the same mouth come both blessing and cursing. My brethren, these things ought not to be this way.* (James 3:5-10)

The expression of anger has been classified into two categories: *passive* anger and *active* anger. The passive category includes *malice, hatred, bitterness, resentment, unforgiveness, jealousy, envy, exasperation, frustration, irritation, annoyance,* and *silent repression.* The active category includes *murder, suicide, rage, violence, bullying, slander, excluding, provoking, humiliating, gossip, ridicule, sarcasm,* and *criticism.* These are the very things that God's Word commands that we are to put away (Ephesians 4:31).

Expressions of anger in both the passive and the active categories are sinful. One group internalizes anger and the other spews it out with vengeance. Both are unbiblical ways of dealing with anger.

Sinful Anger
There are two kinds of anger: *righteous* anger and *sinful* anger. Since all anger is *not* sinful, how can we know when our anger is sinful? Sinful anger is horrible, hellish, and hurtful. It must be discerned and condemned; how can we differentiate between a righteous anger and sinful anger? The following distinctives will help to identify sinful anger accurately and biblically.

Anger is sinful when it is unjustified. "*I say to you that whosoever is angry with his brother without a cause is in danger of the judgment*" (Matthew 5:22, KJV). Unjustified anger is a product of a selfish, self-absorbed, idolatrous heart. Justifiable anger toward a person is rare. John Piper writes:

> [Anger] devours almost all other good emotions. It deadens the soul. It numbs the heart to joy and gratitude and hope and tenderness and compassion and kindness." [5]

Anger is sinful when it is unforgiving. Consider carefully what Christ said: "*If you forgive others for their transgressions, your heavenly Father will also forgive you. But if you do not forgive others, then your Father will not forgive your transgressions"* (Matthew 6:14-15). Regardless of how you interpret these verses, one thing is clear, to be unforgiving is sinful. If you find within yourself anger and unforgiveness, you must, according to Scripture, examine whether or not YOU are a forgiven sinner. Are you thinking, "You don't understand what wrongs and wounds have been done to me?" It really doesn't matter; if you are angry and cannot forgive, your anger is sinful. That is not to say that what was done to you is OK. Even if the act against you was wrong and sinful, you cannot hold unforgiveness and fermenting anger in your heart without causing ruinous damage within and without. Those hurts must be dealt with scripturally.

Anger is sinful when there is an absence of love. If your anger toward another person keeps you from expressing genuine godly love toward that person, then your anger falls into the category of Vengeance, and that is sinful. Paul quoting from Deuteronomy 32:35 wrote, *"Vengeance is Mine, I will repay," says the Lord"* (Romans 12:19). You have heard people jokingly say "I don't get angry, I get even"; but don't be quick to laugh. That's the attitude condemned by Scripture. Don't laugh at anything that God wouldn't laugh at.

Anger is sinful when it is unresolved. When anger is not resolved, it becomes a welcomed emotion. Some people are actually delighted that they have anger toward other people—they actually enjoy being angry, and often label it as "righteous." When people become angry over something in their church and decide to go to another church, they take their anger with them. Sadly, this unresolved anger will likely sprout and take root in the new church. Anger must be dealt with scripturally; a change of scenery never uproots Anger. Don't be a carrier!

Anger is sinful when it is unbridled. When someone perceives that they are the object of injustice, the natural reaction is to tell somebody off. That's what the world would advise: "Go tell them off.

You owe it to yourself. You don't owe them anything—you have to look out for number one, you know. Stand up for your rights!" The Lord addressed this in the book of James, *"If anyone thinks himself to be religious, and yet does not bridle his tongue but deceives his own heart, this man's religion is worthless"* (James 1:26).

Take a close look at a man who became consumed with sinful Anger. His anger was unjustified, unforgiving, unloving, unresolved, and unbridled (untamed); that man was Cain. *"And the LORD had regard for Abel and for his offering; but for Cain and for his offering He had no regard. So Cain became very angry and his countenance fell"* (Genesis 4:4-5).

First, the Source of Cain's anger was the Sovereignty of God. The central issue facing man is WHO IS BOSS. Who is in charge? Who occupies the throne? Who has sovereign rights over the events of life? This issue comes into play each time God's will and my will, my life, my dreams, my ambitions, and desires face each other. This is what happened with Cain. Adam and Eve had, without doubt, taught their sons that a blood sacrifice was God's means to approach Him. However, Cain rejected that way. Cain had his own ideas about worship and acceptance with God. Be very, very careful with the things of God. He abhors man's *personal preferences*, He accepts only what He Himself prescribes. Cain brought some vegetables to the altar, the produce of his own labor. Cain's will clashed with God's will and, as usual, God wins. The animal sacrifice of Abel is accepted; the vegetable sacrifice of Cain is rejected. Anger burned and seethed within Cain, and eventually consumed him.

Being religious was not the issue. The issue was who was going to call the shots, Cain or God. Cain's problem was self-determination, or selfishness, which is the root of sinful anger. Cain sat on the throne of Cain's heart.

Second, the Sustainer of Cain's anger was Stubbornness (Genesis. 4:4-7). Cain was so stubborn he would not consider changing. Cain wanted to worship Cain's way and he wanted God to be pleased with what pleased Cain. When you see a person who is so stubborn they refuse change, even if commanded by God, you are looking at an angry person. Cain became so angry it showed in his face, *"So Cain became very angry and his countenance fell"* (Genesis 4:5). I have actually heard people say, "I know what the Bible says, but I am not going to do it that way." Such a person has anger in their heart toward God. They are rebellious and so stubborn that they will not change until or unless the Holy Spirit brings them down.

Third, the Significance of Cain's anger was Devastating (Genesis 4:4-15). What were the consequences, the significance, and the end result of Cain's anger? Nothing is without consequence and sinful anger explodes with consequences.

Cain became vulnerable to open sin. The Lord clearly warned Cain, *"If you do well, will not your countenance be lifted up? And if you do not do well, sin is crouching at the door; and its desire is for you, but you must master it"* (Genesis 4:7). Because his anger was so strong, his countenance fell, and Cain stood with open arms to sin. You cannot harbor sinful anger without making yourself vulnerable to even more sinful emotions and acts.

Cain's heart became filled with vengeance and hatred (Genesis 4:8) He began to vent his hatred and anger toward his brother rather than toward a solution. Jealousy, selfishness with a vengeance, took control of Cain's mind. A Cain controlled by sinful anger now sat on the throne of Cain's heart.

Rage gives birth to murder (Genesis 4:8). His anger, jealousy, selfishness, and vengeance were so great that he actually murdered his own brother. Christ equated sinful anger with murder (Matthew 5:21-23).

Cain lost his integrity; he began to lie. *"Then the Lord said to Cain, 'Where is Abel your brother'? And he said, 'I do not know, am I my brother's keeper?"* (Genesis 4:9). The Lord was not seeking information. He knew quite well what had happened to Abel; He was confronting Cain about his murderous deed. Instead of confessing his sins and telling the truth, he spoke arrogantly and lied to the Lord.

Judgment always follows murderous anger (Genesis 4:10-15). Whether it be temporal or eternal judgment, God always has consequences when someone harbors sinful anger in their heart. While God may forgive sin, He does not always remove consequences from our sins. For example, a person may drink enough alcohol to cause liver damage—God may deliver that person from the addiction, but He does not always remove the consequence.

Fear is another consequence of Cain's anger (Genesis 4:14). Cain lived the remainder of his life in fear and rejection. He was always looking over his shoulder, constantly moving from one place to another. He could never have peace or get a good night's sleep.

You see, sinful anger—anger that is unjustified, unforgiving, unloving, unresolved, and unbridled—will destroy you. It must be dealt with and it must be dealt with according to the Scriptures. There are at least five things a Christian can do to deal with anger scripturally.

First, give thanks. "See that no one repays another with evil for evil, but always seek after that which is good for one another and for all people. Rejoice always; pray without ceasing; **in everything give thanks***; for this is God's will for you in Christ Jesus"* (1 Thessalonians 5:15-18, emphasis mine).

God is sovereign and He either causes or allows events for a purpose. As a Christian, events are designed to focus you on Christ, mature you in the faith, and ultimately glorify God. Therefore, you must learn to give thanks even though you do not always see or understand the purpose behind the events. Need help? Ask Him to give you what He commands. "Whether we like it or not, asking is the rule of His Kingdom." [6]

Second, confess—not repress—your sinful anger. If you do not confess your sin, you are not forgiven of that sin. Repressed sinful anger only reproduces itself and leads to more sin. Blow up or clam up—both are wrong. Repressed anger can quickly lead to several things, such as lashing out at the innocent, discouragement, severe stress, and depression.

Third, consider your sinful anger. Analyze scripturally what you are thinking and doing; consider the consequences of your anger. *"He who is slow to wrath has great understanding, but he who is impulsive exalts folly"* (Proverbs 14:29, NKJV). Generally when we think through what or who we are angry with, we can find a solution without sinfully venting that anger. We are also reminded by the Scriptures, *"Everyone must be quick to hear, slow to speak and slow to anger"* (James 1:19-20).

Fourth, you must learn to control your anger. *"A fool vents all his feelings, but a wise man holds them back"* (Proverbs 19:11). Anger is a God-given emotion. But when we don't control anger, anger controls us and is sinful. Sinful Anger isn't submissive; it is always causing something bad. When anything gets between a Self-heart and its pleasures, beware! Wicked anger is an assassin sent from the throne room of the Self-heart. For the Christian, Christ must reign on the heart throne. Christ demands ALL, and can rightfully do so, for He is the Creator and King. Satan will gladly have whatever is yielded to him, however small a portion of the life, heart, or mind it may be, for he knows that Christ will have ALL or NONE! Who's on your heart throne?

Fifth, direct your anger toward the problem or event which caused your rage and seek a solution rather than revenge. Directing sinful anger toward a person compounds the problem and transforms what may be an angry heart into a raging vengeful heart.

Good Anger

Good anger is quite simple. Good anger has love for God and the things of God as its motive. Good anger is always directed toward an act, not a person. It is the motivation to solve a problem, not create one. It seeks to right a wrong. It is zealous for the truth of God and the glory of God. When our Lord became angry, it was because of man's sinful acts; He took action to solve the problem. We do not have the authority to drive people out of the temple, but we do have the authority and responsibility to go to the person and make an attempt to right the wrong they are doing or have done.

There is one other Proverb I would like to briefly mention.

> *Do not associate with a man given to anger;*
> *or go with a hot-tempered man,*
> *or you will learn his ways and find a snare for yourself.*
> (Proverbs 22:24-25)

Generally speaking, no one wants to be around a person who is hot-tempered and angry most of the time. They don't make very good company and they certainly bring no glory to God. The Proverb warns that if we spend a lot of time around an angry person, we will become like him.

"BE ANGRY, and yet DO NOT SIN; do not let the sun go down on your anger. And do not give the devil an opportunity" (Ephesians 4:26-27, emphasis mine). Cain gave place to the devil and it destroyed him. This passage in Ephesians addresses at least two important things. We are to be angry about certain things and we are to seek an immediate solution if possible. We should be angry at injustices, sin, and acts that dishonor our Lord. But righteous anger drives us to pray and work for scriptural and Christ-honoring solutions.

> Righteous wrath is no less noble than love,
> since both coexist in God. [7]

Unfortunately, I have to say that most angry people are angry at the Lord, as was Cain, and the actions and bitter fruits are felt most by the people around them, those that love them the most. Many a sweet child has fallen victim to an angry parent, not because of acting like a child, but because they were the nearest when Anger was given opportunity to erupt against a helpless heart. Ultimately sinful wrath rears its Medusa head when Self doesn't get what Self wants. Self thinks it deserves better than what God has given or allowed. Sometimes the Lord gives a person the consequences of his bad choices and his rebellious heart rages.

> *The foolishness of man ruins his way,*
> *And his heart rages against the Lord.*
> (Proverbs 19:3)

And since they can't get at God to vent their anger, they take it out on those closest to them.

Sinful and unjustified anger flourishes most rapidly in the heart that idolizes itself, is ungrateful, selfish, and un-submissive to God. If that person is you, confess this wretched sin and surrender immediately to the will of Christ, seek forgiveness and the Great Physician's healing. Regardless of the circumstances at the core of your anger, surrender to Him and trust His heart of love for you.

> Do not say "I cannot help having a bad temper." Friend, you must help it. Pray to God to help you overcome it at once, for either you must kill it or it will kill you. You cannot carry a bad temper into Heaven. [8]

Unrighteous anger scoffs at the Word of God and will plunge its host into the blackness of DarkLand. Don't let that be you. Take to heart what Paul wrote: *"We know that God causes all things to work together for good to those who love God, to those who are called according to His purpose"* (Romans 8:28). There is freedom from anger by casting yourself upon that verse every day and every night. Trust Christ as your great Physician who has power and willingness and desire to heal your heart. Yield to His medicines.

---

1. Henry Drummond (1851-1897), www.worldofquotes.com/author/henry+drummond/1/index.html
2. Minirth & Meyer, *Happiness is a Choice*, Baker Books, 1994, p. 112
3. C.S. Lewis, poietes.wordpress.com
4. Matthew Henry, *Commentary on the Whole Bible*, Vol. VI, p. 707
5. *This Momentary Marriage: A Parable of Permanence*, Desiring God Foundation, 2008, p. 150 (www.desiringgod.org)
6. *The Prayer Life of the Spiritual Leaders*, March 18, 2006, (www.beliefnet.com/...spurgeon)
7. John MacAarthur, *The Book on Leadership*, Wolgemuth & Assoc, Inc., 2004, p. 204
8. Charles Spurgeon (christian-quotes-ochristian.com)

16

THE KING SAYS COME

Come to Me, all who are weary and heavy-laden, and I will give you rest. Take My yoke upon you and learn from Me, for I am gentle and humble in heart, and you will find rest for your souls. For My yoke is easy and My burden is light. (Matthew 11:28-30)

The problems addressed in this book are common to all people, including Christ's own beloved ones, those who call themselves by His Name—Christians. Because of our fallen sinful nature and God's great purpose, which has brought us from death into life, Christians wrestle with things that must be cut from and pulled from our hearts and minds; everything that wars against His goal for us must go. Our path at times is flooded with light and restful gifts from Him. But it is rare that those times last for very long. Our armor is employed and our dependence on our King is exercised and sharpened in adversity and affliction. We fall into the mire and maze of DarkLand where we learn to trust and use our weapons. We must not lay our weapons down and wallow in our circumstances.

There is relief and solution in the Person and Work of the Lord Jesus Christ. Tragically in our postmodern world people don't want to consider God, much less biblical solutions. Mocking Him and His Word is the bent of our society. Calling out to stressed and discouraged people, the world beckons the wounded to go down *any* path to *anything* - except the *one* way that leads to genuine truth, solutions, peace, and life, which is Christ and His Word.

After preaching to a group of villagers in Ukraine a few years ago, I was approached by a man who, from the smell of his breath, was obviously intoxicated. He informed me that he had two demons with which he wanted me do deal. When I inquired as to what his demons were, he responded "alcohol and smoking." I spoke to him about the gospel of Jesus Christ, sin, repentance, and submission to the claims of the Lord Jesus Christ. But that wasn't the answer he wanted to hear. By using the term demon I suppose he wanted me to do some kind of exorcism to get the demons out of him so he could go on his way. I'm not sure what he really wanted, but I am sure that he didn't want to hear what I told him. He went away grumbling and murmuring to himself.

His response was the same as millions of other people. They live a life of ignorance or disobedience to the Word of God. But when the consequences of their desires and actions manifest themselves in their life they look for the "quick fix." They don't want to hear about the God who claims and demands all.

The world can no more give peace and answers than a thorn bush can give you grapes. DarkLand is filled with the thorn bushes of False Promise—you reach in to grasp what looks good, but come out with pain, cuts, and infection. The Word of God gives real answers, but sadly even Christians have to learn the hard way that the only thorn bush that provides answers and peace was woven into a cruel crown and pressed into the head of the Prince of Peace. Our crown, on His head; our nails, in His hands and feet; His blood, our salvation, healing, peace, and joy. The King Himself speaks:

> *Come to Me, all who are weary and heavy-laden, and I will give you rest. Take My yoke upon you and learn from Me, for I am gentle and humble in heart, and YOU WILL FIND REST FOR YOUR SOULS.*

> *For My yoke is easy and My burden is light.* (Matthew 11:28-30, emphasis mine)

The King says COME. Christ who is the sovereign King over the souls and affairs of men says "Come." He is the God-man who came into His own creation clothed in human flesh. He is the one who lived among men for thirty-three years, experiencing all the things men face, sin excepted. He is the One who took upon Himself the crushing sins of His people and the penalty of justice and wrath demanded of a Holy God. Lifted toward heaven on the cross of pain and suffering, He endured the wrath of God for those sins. His own Father turned away; He suffered alone. *"My God, My God, why have you forsaken Me."* That, dear soul, is the price and cost of all the good that flows from His call to "Come." All sin will be punished either in the death of Christ as the Substitute, or, in the case of the sinner without Christ, payment will be exacted for eternity in hell separated from an offended God. Dietrich Bonhoeffer, theologian, pastor, and martyr, was a faithful servant of Christ in Germany during the rise and power of Adolph Hitler. Bonhoeffer wrote:

> Cheap grace is the deadly enemy of our Church. We are fighting today for costly grace…
>
> Costly grace is the treasure hidden in the field; for the sake of it a man will gladly go and sell all that he has. It is the pearl of great price for which the merchant will sell all his goods. It is the kingly rule of Christ, for Whose sake a man will pluck out the eye which causes him to stumble. It is the call of Jesus Christ at which the disciple leaves his nets and follows Him.
>
> Costly grace is the gospel which must be sought again and again and again, the gift which must be

asked for, the door at which a man must knock. Such grace is costly because it calls us to follow, and it is grace because it calls us to follow Jesus Christ.

It is costly because it costs a man his life,
and it is grace because it gives a man the only true life.

It is costly because it condemns sin,
and grace because it justifies the sinner.

Above all, it is costly because it cost God the life of His Son: "Ye were bought at a price," and what has cost God much cannot be cheap for us.

Above all, it is grace because God did not reckon His Son too dear a price to pay for our life, but delivered Him up for us. Costly grace is the Incarnation of God. [1]

It is *that* King who bids you "COME!"

The King INVITES "all who are weary and heavy-laden," all who are suffering in any manner whether physical, emotional, or spiritual, all who are discouraged, all who are depressed, all who are stressed, all who have no patience with suffering, all who are afraid, all who are grieving, all who are being persecuted for righteousness sake, all who are weighted down with guilt, all who are in need of recognition, and all who are struggling with anger. These are the people who are heavy-laden and these are the people who are invited.

The King Gives a PROMISE: "and I will give you rest." He may not always take away the suffering, but He gives something far better—Himself. He will give you the grace to endure it and a Rest in Him.

He did not take away Paul's thorn, but He gave him grace to endure it (2 Corinthians 12). Infirmities may be banished, or confirmed as needful for you at the time. This is not the promise of some mere man, but it is the promise of the Lord of Glory who has the ability to make good on His promises.

> *Do not fear, for I am with you;*
> *Do not anxiously look about you, for I am your God.*
> *I will strengthen you, surely I will help you.*
> *Surely I will uphold you with My righteous right hand.*
> (Isaiah 41:10)

The King Instructs Us in His School. Once we come to Him in surrender, faith, and submission, He tells us to *"Take My yoke upon you and learn from Me..."* We are to become disciples—learners of Christ. The more we learn from Him, the more we will be like Him; as soldiers, we are trained by the Captain of our salvation. We are inexorably joined to One Who has all power, all love, and is *for us*. Although we are slow learners and have no abilities in ourselves, we cannot fail. Our Teacher gives us His Word, interprets it to us, and then throws us into the battle to make His lessons real in us.

The signposts and warning lights in DarkLand will make our path more clear and bright. The King of the land sets His guards and guides all around us for we are His own, His children, His beloved ones.

He tells us that His yoke is not harsh or burdensome: *"for I am gentle and humble in heart, and you will find rest for your souls. For My yoke is easy and My burden is light."* When we come to Him there is peace with God, no condemnation, and our burdens are lifted; we find rest. The yoke of the Lord is our place of maturity and delight. His Word will be precious, prayer our joy, we will drink in the preached word as the water and medicine of life, we will find shelter and strength in the fellowship of His Spirit and His people.

The Apostle Peter directs us, *"casting all your anxiety on Him, because He cares for you"* (1 Peter 5:7). That, dear soul, is the greatest advice. Take heart, for there is help in the Lord Jesus Christ. Like children, we learn, grow, and mature. It is His business to care for us and provide whatever is necessary to bring the diamonds out of the lumps of coal. The King never forgets His business.

> *I will be their God, and they shall be my people.*
> (Hebrews 8:10)

> He who has God to be his God—cannot lack any good thing; but he who has not God for his God—lacks everything really and truly good.
>
> If Jehovah is your God—then *all his glorious perfections* are engaged and employed for your welfare: His *mercy* will supply all your needs; His *power* will conquer all your foes; His *wisdom* will direct your way; His *faithfulness* will answer your prayers; His *justice* will maintain your cause; and His *infinite love and grace* will be displayed in all His dealings with you!
>
> If God is your God, then...His *promises*—are your heritage, His *precepts*—are your rule, His *doctrines*—are your present paradise, His *Son*—is your Savior and King, His *Spirit*—is your Sanctifier and Tutor, and He Himself—is your everlasting portion!
>
> If God is your God, then He will freely confer on you all good things at present—and crown you at last with everlasting glory. He will...guide you continu-

ally, chasten you occasionally, receive you generously, and bless you indeed!

If God is your God, then all things are yours; things present, things to come; life, death, the world—all are yours.

If God is your God, then all the resources of eternity and all the treasures of time—will, if necessary, be employed in your spiritual and eternal benefit. This is the highest point of blessedness and honor—and this honor have all His saints. [2]

> Jesus, I my cross have taken,
> All to leave and follow Thee.
> Destitute, despised, forsaken,
> Thou from hence my all shall be.
> Perish every fond ambition,
> All I've sought or hoped or known.
> Yet, how rich is my condition!
> God and heaven are still my own.
>
> Let the world despise and leave me,
> They have left my Savior, too.
> Human hearts and looks deceive me;
> Thou art not, like man, untrue.
> And while Thou dost smile upon me,
> God of wisdom, love, and might,
> Foes may hate and friends may shun me,
> Show Thy face and all is bright.
>
> Hasten on from grace to glory,
> Armed by faith and winged by prayer;
> Heaven's eternal days before me,

God's own hand shall guide me there.
Soon shall close my earthly mission,
Swift shall pass my pilgrim days;
Hope shall change to glad fruition,
Faith to sight and prayer to praise. [3]

---

1 Dietrich Bonhoeffer, *The Cost of Discipleship*, Macmillan, 1963, pp. 45-47
2 James Smith, gracegems.org/d/smith.htm
3 Henry Francis Lyte (1793-1847), *Jesus, I My Cross Have Taken*, Hymn # 321, The New Church Hymnal, Lexicon Music, Inc., Newbury Park, California

Ed Wallen is now retired after nearly fifty-five years in pastoral ministry. During those years he pastored in Germany, Kentucky and Alabama. He is the founder and president of Bible Study Foundation which sponsored a ministry in Ukraine where he taught theology to pastors and assisted in the formation of new churches. He presently spends his time writing and producing *Think Scripturally,* a weekly email devotion. He and his wife Tommie reside in Alabaster, Alabama.